Troubleshooting OpenVPN

Get the solutions you need to troubleshoot any issue you may face to keep your OpenVPN up and running

Eric F Crist

BIRMINGHAM - MUMBAI

Troubleshooting OpenVPN

First published: March 2017

Production reference: 1150317

Published by Packt Publishing Ltd.
Livery Place
35 Livery Street
Birmingham
B3 2PB, UK.
ISBN 978-1-78646-196-4

www.packtpub.com

Credits

Author
Eric F Crist

Reviewer
Krzee King

Commissioning Editor
Pratik Shah

Acquisition Editor
Divya Poojari

Content Development Editor
Abhishek Jadhav

Technical Editor
Gaurav Suri

Copy Editor
Dipti Mankame

Project Coordinator
Judie Jose

Proofreader
Safis Editing

Indexer
Pratik Shirodkar

Graphics
Kirk D'Penha

Production Coordinator
Shantanu N. Zagade

About the Author

Eric F Crist hails from Cottage Grove, Minnesota, and he works as a product and systems engineer for Abbott. He has a relatively wide range of professional and life experience starting from physical security and access control as a low-voltage technician into software development, system administration, and software development.

Eric has been a core member of the OpenVPN community since 2008 and helps manage the open source online resources. He also wrote ssl-admin, and he is a lead for Easy-RSA, both of which help manage Certificate Authorities and chains.

Eric collaborated with Jan Just Keisjer for the book, *Mastering OpenVPN*, in 2015, also for Packt.

I would like to sincerely thank my wife, DeeDee, for encouraging me to write this book. Without your prompting, encouragement, and motivation, I would have had a tremendous amount of additional free time and sanity.

About the Reviewer

Krzee King is a self taught BSD/Linux user. He began helping in the OpenVPN community in 2007, when he and the author Eric took control of the IRC channel, and later founded the web forum with Eric and *dougy*. He believes very strongly in the importance of encryption, and the need for strong encryption to be usable by all. He also had the pleasure of reviewing *OpenVPN 2 Cookbook* by Jan Just Keijser.

Thanks to my lovely wife and my parents, for their endless support. I love you guys.

www.PacktPub.com

For support files and downloads related to your book, please visit www.PacktPub.com.

Did you know that Packt offers eBook versions of every book published, with PDF and ePub files available? You can upgrade to the eBook version at www.PacktPub.com and as a print book customer, you are entitled to a discount on the eBook copy. Get in touch with us at service@packtpub.com for more details.

At www.PacktPub.com, you can also read a collection of free technical articles, sign up for a range of free newsletters and receive exclusive discounts and offers on Packt books and eBooks.

https://www.packtpub.com/mapt

Get the most in-demand software skills with Mapt. Mapt gives you full access to all Packt books and video courses, as well as industry-leading tools to help you plan your personal development and advance your career.

Why subscribe?

- Fully searchable across every book published by Packt
- Copy and paste, print, and bookmark content
- On demand and accessible via a web browser

Customer Feedback

Thanks for purchasing this Packt book. At Packt, quality is at the heart of our editorial process. To help us improve, please leave us an honest review on this book's Amazon page at `https://www.amazon.com/dp/178646196X`.

If you'd like to join our team of regular reviewers, you can e-mail us at `customerreviews@packtpub.com`. We award our regular reviewers with free eBooks and videos in exchange for their valuable feedback. Help us be relentless in improving our products!

Table of Contents

Preface

OpenVPN is arguably the best cross-platform secure networking technology currently available. The development community is large and active every day of the year, with new developers popping up regularly with patches and feature requests. It is not only used by hobbyists, but also by for-pay VPN providers strewn about the Internet.

In *Troubleshooting OpenVPN*, we identify the most common problems and pitfalls in the deployment of OpenVPN. We demonstrate where and how to use an assortment of diagnostic and investigative tools, both common and lesser known.

By the end of this book, you should be able to understand and identify where a problem resides, both within your VPN infrastructure and also from external causes. The log file is fully detailed and you will be able to leverage the varying logging levels to suit your troubleshooting efforts.

What this book covers

Chapter 1, *Troubleshooting Basics*, helps the reader break down problems into digestible portions with related components. Some of the concepts discussed include generic techniques useful in more than just OpenVPN problem solving.

Chapter 2, *Common Problems*, will identify the issues seen most frequently by both novice administrators and experienced administrators alike.

Chapter 3, *Installing OpenVPN*, covers compilation and installation of OpenVPN on a variety of platforms. Virtual network adapters, alternative client packages, and software dependencies will be identified.

Chapter 4, *The Log File*, focuses heavily on the OpenVPN log file and how to adjust and decipher the verbosity of the available messages. This is an extremely valuable resource when identifying and correcting problems.

Chapter 5, *Client and Server Startup*, discusses software and system dependencies necessary for process startup. Items like file permissions, scripting, and basic networking all contribute to successfully running OpenVPN.

Chapter 6, *Certificates and Authentication*, illustrates the varying authentication paths and where breakage can occur. System time, authentication backends and scripting are all addressed.

`Chapter 7`, *Network and Routing*, shows where network topology and routing bring complexity to the OpenVPN architecture. Conflicting routes, address inconsistency, and subnetting will all be covered.

`Chapter 8`, *Performance*, was written to help you identify performance bottlenecks and places where efficiencies can be improved.

`Chapter 9`, *External Problems*, covers where and when problems can exist outside your OpenVPN infrastructure, and even entirely outside your network or control.

What you need for this book

This book was written with the VPN administrator in mind. Many of the examples within leverage both the server and client sides of a connection, and lack of control at the server end will prove frustrating. I am assuming you either have access to a server, or have the means to create a functioning server, with your operating system of choice.

Examples within this book are focused primarily on Linux or BSD command-line tools, but there are a number of Windows examples interspersed within the content. To make the most of your time, try to have the following available:

- An OpenVPN server, ideally running on Linux or FreeBSD
- An OpenVPN client, running any operating system you choose
- The ability to install software on and connect to the OpenVPN server without OpenVPN running

Who this book is for

An OpenVPN server administrator is most likely to use this book to its potential. Enterprising VPN users may also be able to use the techniques and applications described within to their own benefit, however. Much of this title covers basic troubleshooting skills that can be leveraged in nearly any situation, not just with OpenVPN.

Conventions

In this book, you will find a number of text styles that distinguish between different kinds of information. Here are some examples of these styles and an explanation of their meaning.

Code words in text, database table names, folder names, filenames, file extensions, pathnames, dummy URLs, user input, and Twitter handles are shown as follows: "The `--auth-user-pass-verify` script is the last in a long chain of scripts that are run."

Any command-line input or output is written as follows:

```
author@example:~-> sudo openssl s_server -key key.pem -cert cert.pem -WWW -
accept 443
```

New terms and **important words** are shown in bold. Words that you see on the screen, for example, in menus or dialog boxes, appear in the text like this: "By going to **Preferences** | **Protocols** | **SSL**, Wireshark provides a way to import the TLS key we created earlier."

Warnings or important notes appear in a box like this.

Tips and tricks appear like this.

Reader feedback

Feedback from our readers is always welcome. Let us know what you think about this book-what you liked or disliked. Reader feedback is important for us as it helps us develop titles that you will really get the most out of. To send us general feedback, simply e-mail feedback@packtpub.com, and mention the book's title in the subject of your message. If there is a topic that you have expertise in and you are interested in either writing or contributing to a book, see our author guide at www.packtpub.com/authors.

Customer support

Now that you are the proud owner of a Packt book, we have a number of things to help you to get the most from your purchase.

Errata

Although we have taken every care to ensure the accuracy of our content, mistakes do happen. If you find a mistake in one of our books-maybe a mistake in the text or the code-we would be grateful if you could report this to us. By doing so, you can save other readers from frustration and help us improve subsequent versions of this book. If you find any errata, please report them by visiting `http://www.packtpub.com/submit-errata`, selecting your book, clicking on the **Errata Submission Form** link, and entering the details of your errata. Once your errata are verified, your submission will be accepted and the errata will be uploaded to our website or added to any list of existing errata under the Errata section of that title.

To view the previously submitted errata, go to `https://www.packtpub.com/books/content/support`and enter the name of the book in the search field. The required information will appear under the **Errata** section.

Piracy

Piracy of copyrighted material on the Internet is an ongoing problem across all media. At Packt, we take the protection of our copyright and licenses very seriously. If you come across any illegal copies of our works in any form on the Internet, please provide us with the location address or website name immediately so that we can pursue a remedy.

Please contact us at `copyright@packtpub.com` with a link to the suspected pirated material.

We appreciate your help in protecting our authors and our ability to bring you valuable content.

Questions

If you have a problem with any aspect of this book, you can contact us at `questions@packtpub.com`, and we will do our best to address the problem.

1
Troubleshooting Basics

Troubleshooting a failed server or client deployment can be a daunting task, particularly for a novice user. A vast number of users do not fall into the typical system administration role, and they are either hobbyists or just venturing into virtual networking and cryptography. By the end of this chapter, the tools' key to identifying and correcting problems will be illustrated, and their utility will be demonstrated.

The general concepts of troubleshooting apply not only to fixing a problematic **OpenVPN** client or server process but also to nearly everything encountered in day-to-day work. At its most basic level, the idea of *divide and conquer* is the phrase of the day. Separating components that are functional from those that are broken will quickly absolve the administrator from needless work and investigation.

The book is structured progressively, and it aims to help you find solutions quickly. This book will cover the following key topics surrounding fixing, identifying, and resolving OpenVPN problems:

- A troubleshooting toolkit is a key to gleaning all the data needed to focus on a problem and resolve it.
- Common OpenVPN issues are explored. Years of help supporting OpenVPN administrators on the forums and in IRC have provided a plethora of data, and the most common issues faced in the field are identified and solutions are provided.
- The OpenVPN installation on various operating systems is covered. The best client for each operating system is identified, including mobile device options. Where to go to obtain the installers and files needed.
- Log files are the primary source of troubleshooting data. When to use what verbosity level and how to search for the data within the log is explained.

- Startup and shutdown of the OpenVPN process for both the client and the server can cause stress and anguish. OpenVPN packaging is explained, where to go for help is shown, and how to troubleshoot those startup routines will be demonstrated.
- Routing and networking can be a difficult concept to comprehend. This is likely the number one area of difficulty for beginning OpenVPN administrators.
- We will discuss performance issues and how to correct performance-related issues. Also, cipher suite, key size, compression, and routing optimization will be illustrated.
- Finally, problems external to OpenVPN will be explored. Such things include local LAN address collisions and incorrect firewall filtering, both locally and at an ISP.

A recommended toolkit

There are a number of common utilities needed to investigate network and **public key infrastructure** (**PKI**) issues. The samples within this book will be from a variety of operating systems. The server will be on FreeBSD 10.2, and we will show macOS X and Windows 7 and 10.

The majority of diagnostics will be done at the server side of the connection, but there are useful things to glean from client-side utilities. The tools listed here will be demonstrated, but this book isn't a manual for their use. For full documentation, refer to the documentation links provided.

 Both the FreeBSD project and GNU have web interfaces for browsing man pages. The main page for these can be found at the following paths:

- **FreeBSD**: https://www.freebsd.org/cgi/man.cgi
- **GNU**: http://www.gnu.org/manual/manual.en.html

Log search and filtering

Detailed logging is available from OpenVPN on both the client and server sides, which allows configuration issues to be identified quickly. Having the ability to search these logs for the pertinent information is vital to successfully correcting problems and verifying a functional service. The utilities identified here will aid in these search tasks.

grep

The `grep` utility is likely to be one of the first utilities learned by an aspiring Unix user. Finding strings or keywords within a file or a set of files quickly is the first step in tracking down entries in a log file or a configuration directive. `grep` allows you to search and highlight specific lines, context around those lines, filenames, line numbers, and more. In addition to finding lines of text, `grep` can also omit lines you do not want to see.

The *#openvpn* support channel on **Freenode** (`irc.freenode.net`) IRC as well as on the OpenVPN forum (`http://forums.openvpn.net`), for example, request that users seeking support omit comments and empty lines with the following command:

```
grep -vE '^#|^;|^$' server.conf
```

Take a sample config file:

```
ecrist@meow:~-> cat foo.conf
# this is a comment
; this is also a comment

# the line above is empty

config argument

; another comment
```

If we pipe that through our `grep` filter:

```
ecrist@meow:~-> grep -vE '^#|^;|^$' foo.conf
config argument
```

less, more, and most

Paging applications are a common feature of Unix and Unix-like operating systems. These tools allow the user to view a large amount of content, typically text, to be viewed one page at a time. In general, there are three such common tools, `less`, `more`, and `most`.

The `more` utility is the most ubiquitous of the three, being installed by default on every Unix, Linux, or other similar system I have used for the past 20 years. Being the first paging utility, the `more` utility's general functionality is limited. When output from a file or pipe contained more content than what could be displayed on a single screen, the content would be paged.

Scrolling down through the content was possible either a line at a time, using a down arrow key press, or a full page/window at a time with a press of the spacebar. Scrolling back up was not supported:

In 1983, Mark Nudelman authored the less utility specifically for backward scroll capability. It was released in May, 1985, via the newsgroup *net.sources*. Many features have been added to less, including pattern match highlighting and *vi*-like movement through the stream. To date, there have been over 450 released updates.

Modern Unix and Linux systems typically ship just the less utility now, with more being a hard-link to the less binary. When executed this way, less operates in a compatibility mode similar to more. This behavior can also be evoked by setting the environment variable LESS_IS_MORE.

The final pager of note is most, which operates similar to less, but adds the capability for multiple windows within a single terminal session. The most pager also appears to support color escape sequences better than less. The following screenshot shows most displaying two windows, one with the less man page and the other with the most man page:

```
                                        author@example
MOST(1)                                                          MOST(1)


NAME
       most - browse or page through a text file

SYNOPSIS
       most  [-1bCcdMstuvwz]  [+lineno]  [+c] [+d] [+s] [+u] [+/string] [file-
       name...]

DESCRIPTION
       most is a paging program that displays, one windowful at  a  time,  the
       contents  of  a file on a terminal.  It pauses after each windowful and
       prints on the window status line the screen the file name, current line
       number, and the percentage of the file so far displayed.

       Unlike  other  paging  programs, most is capable of displaying an arbi-

LESS(1)                                                          LESS(1)


NAME
       less - opposite of more

SYNOPSIS
       less -?
       less --help
       less -V
       less --version
       less [-[+]aABcCdeEfFgGiIJKLmMnNqQrRsSuUVwWX~]
            [-b space] [-h lines] [-j line] [-k keyfile]
            [-[oO] logfile] [-p pattern] [-P prompt] [-t tag]
            [-T tagsfile] [-x tab,...] [-y lines] [-[z] lines]
            [-# shift] [+[+]cmd] [--] [filename]...
       (See  the  OPTIONS section for alternate option syntax with long option
       names.)

Press `Q' to quit, `H' for help, and SPACE to scroll.
```

There are packages for most available for FreeBSD, macOS X, and Linux, but the latest release of most was in 2007, and the development seems to have stalled entirely. The windowed features can be replaced with other tools such as **tmux** and **screen**, which fall outside the scope of this book.

Project pages for the less and most utilities can be found at the following paths:

- less: http://www.greenwoodsoftware.com/less/
- most: http://www.jedsoft.org/most/index.html

Regular expressions

Regular expression (regex) is a syntax that can be leveraged with string or pattern matching. There are already troves of other books and online guides about constructing quality regular expressions, but some basic syntax here will get you started in your troubleshooting endeavors.

This book will primarily use regular expressions in conjunction with the `grep` utility described earlier. Coupling regex with `grep` will allow us to specifically grab or omit lines from a log file. This is particularly useful when looking for specific client errors, or omitting a slew of *noisy* log entries from the view.

Regular expressions are composed of a sequence of pattern matching characters and character classes. Character classes are simply groups of characters or character types.

Some syntax characters to note are as follows:

Character	Example	Description and use

^	`^foo`
	Line must start with `foo`.
	`[^ab]`
	Excludes `a` and `b`.
		Denotes the start of the line. Inside a character class, denotes character exclusion.

$	`foo$` Line must end with `foo`.	Denotes the end of the line.
\	`Hello\.` Line contains `Hello` followed by a period.	Signifies the following character should be interpreted literally. To match a \ character, escape itself: `\\`.
( )	`(foobar)` Groups `foobar` together as a single string.	Start and end of a group.
[ ]	`[0-9a-f]` Matches characters `0` through `9` and `a` through `f`.	Start and end of a character class.
\d	`[\da-f]` Matches characters `0` through `9` and `a` through `f`. Note similarity to previous example.	Matches numeric characters. Same as `[0-9]`.
\w	`^\d\w` Matches `0_foobar` but not `foobar` (line must start with digit).	Matches alphanumeric characters including digits, letters, and the underscore. Same as `[0-9a-fA-F_]`.
\s and \t	`[\w\s]` Matches any word, character, or space character one time.	Matches space and tab, respectively.

.	`foobar.` Matches `foobar` plus any other character. (`foobars`, `foobar1`, `foobar_`, and so on).	A period matches any character.

`{min, max}`	`[0-9a-f]{1,9}`
	Characters 0–9 or a–f must appear at least once, and up to nine times.
	`[\d]{3}`
	Any digit must appear exactly three times, does not have to be the same digit.
		Specifies the minimum and maximum of the previous character or group. When only a single quantity is defined, indicates an exact count.

?	`(foobar)?` `foobar` may or may not appear.	The previous character or group may or may not appear.
+	`\w+` Matches any word character one or more times.	Indicates the previous item (group, character class, or character) must appear at least once, or more.
|	`(ab)|(bc)` Both `ab` and `bc` match.	A separator, like a logical OR.

There are a few online tools that can be used to validate and test your regular expression syntax. This is a good idea as they will demonstrate, graphically, how the changes to your pattern affect what is matched within a string or series of strings. Some of the online tools available online are as follows:

- **Regex Pal**: `http://www.regexpal.com`
- **Regexr**: `http://regexr.com`

For additional reading, I strongly suggest the book commonly referred to as the **camel** book *Programming Perl, 4th Edition*, by Larry Wall. When I am stumped or need to understand how a regular expression is functioning, I find it an invaluable resource and a common reference.

You can also find tutorials and reading by navigating to `http://www.regular-expressions.info`.

Network sniffing and analysis

There will be times when log files and OpenVPN output alone are not enough to identify a problem. It is possible that the issue resides outside of the OpenVPN process or the configuration therein. This could mean that there is a protocol error for some program being encapsulated within the tunnel or there is some upstream issue not readily apparent.

The tools listed here will provide an insight to the protocols and environment around and consuming your OpenVPN setup.

tcpdump

The ultimate command-line network diagnostic tool is the venerable `tcpdump`. `tcpdump` is used to capture network traffic on an interface, and it provides an interface to filter-specific traffic, including unique destination addresses, ports, packet types, protocols, and more. This tool can be used at a very low level to determine **maximum transmission unit** (**MTU**) issues, protocol issues, and many others.

Depending on your level of networking experience, this tool may or may not be directly useful, but packet captures can be sent to more experienced people.

 Do not rule this tool out even if you do not fully understand it yourself.

The following screenshot shows a simple single ping from a test host to Google's `8.8.8.8` DNS resolver IP. We had to use `sudo` as the packet capture requires root privileges on the network interface. Our first command line included option `-A`, which specifies ASCII output and is the unintelligible at the end of each packet info line. The second example shows the same ping without the `-A` option (same screenshot):

```
● ● ●                           author@example
        author@example                        author@example                    +
author@example:~-> sudo tcpdump -A -i xn0 host 8.8.8.8
tcpdump: verbose output suppressed, use -v or -vv for full protocol decode
listening on xn0, link-type EN10MB (Ethernet), capture size 65535 bytes
15:15:11.330053 IP terrance.secure-computing.net > google-public-dns-a.google.com: ICMP echo reque
st, id 44040, seq 0, length 64
E..T}G..@....fMS.......u....V.?O..      2.
.................. !"#$%&'()*+,-./01234567
15:15:11.331025 IP google-public-dns-a.google.com > terrance.secure-computing.net: ICMP echo reply
, id 44040, seq 0, length 64
E..T....9........fMS...u....V.?O..      2.
.................. !"#$%&'()*+,-./01234567
^C
2 packets captured
172 packets received by filter
0 packets dropped by kernel
author@example:~-> sudo tcpdump -i xn0 host 8.8.8.8
tcpdump: verbose output suppressed, use -v or -vv for full protocol decode
listening on xn0, link-type EN10MB (Ethernet), capture size 65535 bytes
15:18:18.769311 IP terrance.secure-computing.net > google-public-dns-a.google.com: ICMP echo reque
st, id 44808, seq 0, length 64
15:18:18.771285 IP google-public-dns-a.google.com > terrance.secure-computing.net: ICMP echo reply
, id 44808, seq 0, length 64
^C
2 packets captured
42 packets received by filter
0 packets dropped by kernel
author@example:~-> ▌
```

A much more detailed introduction to `tcpdump` is available by going to Daniel Miessler's blog at `https://danielmiessler.com/study/tcpdump/`.

traceroute

On Linux, BSD, and macOS X, `traceroute`, or on Windows `tracert`, knowing the path to assorted destinations is a crucial tool. You can quickly ascertain whether traffic is departing the default gateway or a VPN connection. As a bonus, response time to each hop along the path is calculated, which may indicate slow points along the route.

Contrary to the popular belief, these commands are not for hacking or seeing how many people are using a website; you will not improve your K/D ratio in *Call of Duty®*. These are legitimate network diagnostic tools.

Check out the YouTube video by *NextGenHacker101* for a quick laugh at `ht tps://www.youtube.com/watch?v=SXmv8quf_xM`.

For a quick change of pace, here is a screenshot of the `tracert` command from Windows 8. From the output, we can see that there are eight hops between my test Windows 8 system and Google's resolver:

```
Microsoft Windows [Version 6.3.9600]
(c) 2013 Microsoft Corporation. All rights reserved.

C:\Users\ecrist>tracert 8.8.8.8

Tracing route to google-public-dns-a.google.com [8.8.8.8]
over a maximum of 30 hops:

  1    <1 ms    <1 ms    21 ms   192.168.19.1
  2     2 ms     5 ms     2 ms   stpl-dsl-gw14.stpl.qwest.net [207.109.2.14]
  3     2 ms     2 ms     2 ms   stpl-agw1.inet.qwest.net [207.109.3.105]
  4    12 ms    11 ms    17 ms   cer-edge-17.inet.qwest.net [67.14.8.90]
  5    11 ms    11 ms    11 ms   216.111.90.126
  6    12 ms    12 ms    12 ms   209.85.244.1
  7    12 ms    12 ms    13 ms   72.14.237.133
  8    22 ms    22 ms    21 ms   209.85.247.4
  9    21 ms    21 ms    21 ms   72.14.234.81
 10     *        *        *      Request timed out.
 11    21 ms    21 ms    21 ms   google-public-dns-a.google.com [8.8.8.8]

Trace complete.

C:\Users\ecrist>_
```

mtr

My `traceroute` or `mtr` is a utility that combines the functionality of `ping` and `traceroute`. This tool can help illustrate where along a network path latency or packet loss occurs. I still prefer to use `ping` and `traceroute` individually at times, but use `mtr` to quickly identify network connectivity issues.

Both `tcpdump` and `tracert` will stop, by default, after the last hop or a maximum of 30 has been reached. `mtr`, on the other hand, will continue cycling until quit with a *Ctrl + C*. `ping` on **nix* system functions in a similar manner of pinging indefinitely.

Here is a sample output from `mtr` between my test system and the Google website:

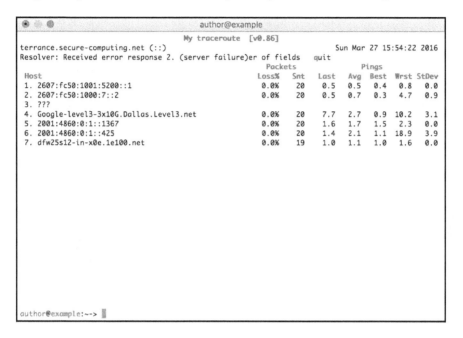

Notice the `Snt` column and that all list `20` apart from hop seven. I pressed *Ctrl* + *C* just as the cycle hit hop seven, so the twentieth packet was never sent.

ping

Good ol' `ping`. This is usually the first tool in the network troubleshooter's toolbox. This is generally the quickest way to determine if a remote system is alive or not. This tool is very much cross-platform, and it is available on Linux, Unix, and Windows systems by default. Only the most hostile or ill-managed corporate networks block this. The following screenshot shows an example of `ping`:

```
author@example:~-> ping -c 4 google.com
PING google.com (216.58.218.174): 56 data bytes
64 bytes from 216.58.218.174: icmp_seq=0 ttl=56 time=0.981 ms
64 bytes from 216.58.218.174: icmp_seq=1 ttl=56 time=1.042 ms
64 bytes from 216.58.218.174: icmp_seq=2 ttl=56 time=1.176 ms
64 bytes from 216.58.218.174: icmp_seq=3 ttl=56 time=18.653 ms

--- google.com ping statistics ---
4 packets transmitted, 4 packets received, 0.0% packet loss
round-trip min/avg/max/stddev = 0.981/5.463/18.653/7.616 ms
author@example:~-> 
```

Wireshark

Coupled with the `tcpdump` utility, and sometimes on its own, **Wireshark** is arguably the most powerful tool in our network troubleshooting toolbox. This tool provides a relatively easy-to-use graphical interface to navigate packet captures. In addition, it provides a filtering interface that allows you to isolate specific streams, protocols, and destinations.

One particular trick Wireshark can do is to decrypt TLS and SSL traffic, given the private and public keys of a web server or server/client pair. This is analogous to the features of the latest *next-generation* firewalls that do decryption at the border for corporate networks.

The following screenshot shows a short eight-packet transaction for a short IPv6 ping:

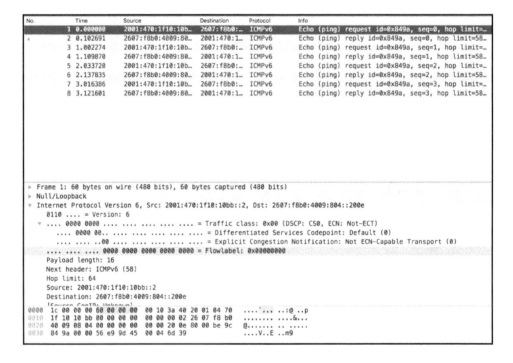

In my experience in the scope of OpenVPN, Wireshark is primarily used along side `tcpdump`. Many OpenVPN servers and clients will have `tcpdump` readily available, already installed, or easily installed when needed. Wireshark requires X11 or other graphical tools and libraries that may not be as easy to install.

It is easy to take a packet capture using `tcpdump`, save the capture to a file (see the `-w` option for `tcpdump`), and transfer that capture to a system with Wireshark installed. The observant reader may have noted the window title in the earlier screenshot: the packet capture here is actually being read-in from a file.

X.509 verification and inspection

Cryptography and PKI are often difficult to understand and much more difficult to resolve issues with. There are primarily two utilities, OpenSSL and Wireshark, that can aid with peering into the cryptographic components of OpenVPN.

 OpenVPN also supports **PolarSSL** (recently known as **ARM® mbed™**) as a replacement for OpenSSL. The latest package, 2.2.1, includes some rudimentary programs for certification creation, but it does not include `s_client` and other utilities included with OpenSSL. More information can be found on their website at `http://tls.mbed.org`.

OpenSSL

OpenSSL is the ubiquitous library for X.509 certificate PKI. OpenVPN has supported the use of X.509 certificates for TLS connections since before 2002. The OpenSSL command-line utilities allow certificate chain verification, outputting certificate details for inspection, build **Diffie-Hellman parameters**, and even substantiating an SSL/TLS server or client instance.

I have used the `s_client` subcommand to fetch the full SSL certification chain for the Google website. All three certificates are listed: the GeoTrust CA root certificate, the Google Intermediate CA (they get to sign their own certificates), and the server certificate their intermediate CA issued. See the following code:

```
author@example:~-> openssl s_client -showcerts -connect openvpn.net:443
```

With this command, I manually copied each certificate block and saved them to individual files, `GoogleSrv.crt` (certificate 0), `GoogleCA.crt` (certificate 1), and `GeoTrustCA.crt` (certificate 2).

A certificate block looks like the following:

```
-----BEGIN CERTIFICATE-----
MIIDfTCCAuagAwIBAgIDErvmMA0GCSqGSIb3DQEBBQUAME4xCzAJBgNVBAYTAlVT
[snip]
NhGc6Ehmo21/uBPUR/6LWlxz/K7ZGzIZOKuXNBSqltLroxwUCEm2u+WR74M26x1W
b8ravHNjkOR/ez4iyz0H7V84dJzjA1BOoa+Y7mHyhD8S
-----END CERTIFICATE-----
```

Wireshark

Wireshark was discussed previously, but this is where that utility will demonstrate its capability. In addition to the ability to decode and illustrate various (nearly all) protocol streams, given the private and public keys available to a VPN admin, it can decipher SSL and TLS encrypted streams, including OpenVPN streams.

To demonstrate the ability to decrypt a TLS session, we will use the OpenSSL `s_server` command to create a generic HTTPS server. I have created a very simple web page that simply reads, **This content is encrypted**. I used the following command to create the server. Note that to start the daemon on port `443`, you need to use root or `sudo`. To avoid escalating privileges, you can use a port `1024`, such as `4443`.

To begin, create a certificate/key pair:

```
author@example:~-> openssl req -x509 -newkey rsa:2048 -keyout
key.pem -out cert.pem -days 365 -nodes
```

Then, we start our server:

```
author@example:~-> sudo openssl s_server -key key.pem -cert
cert.pem -WWW -accept 443
```

The `s_server` process will use the current working directory for its web root, so I placed our web content there as `index.html`.

> The preceding command used `sudo` because it opened a listening port on a privileged port. All TCP/UDP ports numbered `1024` and lower are considered *privileged*, and they require root or administrator permissions to open.

Now, I will start Wireshark and set it to capture traffic on the `loopback` interface. Because we are going to connect to the `localhost` address (`127.0.0.1` or `::1`), the traffic will use this interface. If we connect to the actual system IP address, then capture traffic on the real interface.

Now, open a web browser to the system. In my case, this is the local machine. The URL I will use `https://localhost/index.html`, if you changed the port, add it to the URL such as `https://localhost:4443/index.html`.

If all the steps mentioned earlier were performed correctly, you should have a browser window with a simple message and a Wireshark window with approximately 25 packets captured:

In the packet capture, you will see some protocol data that is indicative of what is happening. We will touch on the protocol exchanges later, but you can clearly see the TLS handshake and cipher exchange taking place:

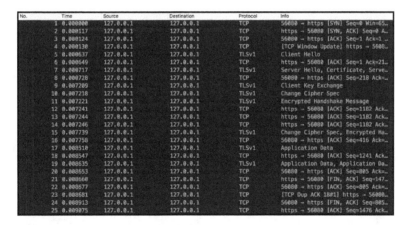

The lines in the capture have a black background, indicating the transmission carried encrypted payload data. Next, we will take the certificate and the key we created earlier and import those into Wireshark. This will allow us to view the transaction.

Before we do that, we will examine packets **17** and **19**. Both of these are labeled with the generic phrase `Application Data` and contain our actual HTML. These packets are encrypted, and they examine them by clicking on them.

By going to **Preferences** | **Protocols** | **SSL**, Wireshark provides a way to import the TLS key we created earlier. On macOS X, the dialog resembles the following screenshot. You can specify the port here, but it is optional. In my case, I simply listed the IP 127.0.0.1 and the key file:

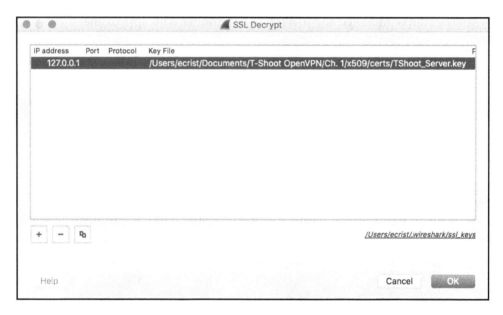

If we go back and inspect our packets now, we can see a new tab in the payload pane. The first is labeled `Frame`, and the second is `Decrypted SSL data`:

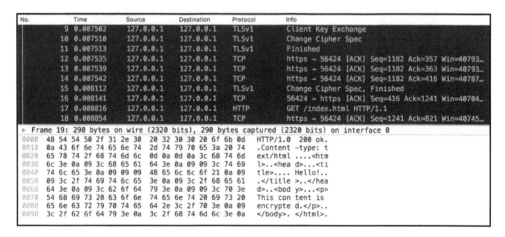

Click on the second tab for packet **19**, and we can actually see the decrypted page content:

```
<html>
    <head>
        <title>
            Hello!
        </title>
    </head>
    <body>
        <p>This content is encrypted.</p>
    </body>
</html>
```

 The ability to decrypt the OpenVPN TLS streams is significant enough that the Wireshark wiki itself has a page specifically demonstrating this capability: https://wiki.wireshark.org/OpenVPN.

Troubleshooting basics

The concept of breaking apart a problem in any system, whether it be electronic, software, physical, or even behavioral, is a common principle. The phrase, *divide and conquer* is often seen, and true to reality.

Readers of this book are likely familiar with the common light bulb. You may not realize it, but there is a series of automatic troubleshooting steps performed.

Imagine the following scenario:

You walk into the office, many are already at work. You step into your office and flip on the light, nothing happens. You flip the switch back and forth a couple times before sitting down and turning on the computer in the dark.

You then pick up the handset on your Cisco IP phone, calling building maintenance. You speak with someone at the other end, exclaiming that the bulbs are out in your office.

What just happened?

A large number of things occurred that weren't directly acknowledged. Most of these steps happened automatically without realization:.

1. Walking into the office. Nothing is out of the ordinary.

   In reality, everyone else was working. There wasn't an uncomfortable silence or notable lack of work or exceptional amount of generalized confusion.

2. You walk in and flip the light switch in your office; more than once.

   You've tried to turn on the light. After the first failure to exhibit illumination, you've automatically tested the switch by flipping it a couple times. Sure, it is not overly scientific, but it's a general functional test.

3. You start working at your own computer, contacting support on your VOIP phone.

   Power works in your office. The computer works, and network PoE is functioning.

4. You've ascertained the only thing not working is the light in your office.

What's neat about this generic situation is many people do so without realizing it. Some have cars and do this when it starts or doesn't start, maybe on a cold morning. Maybe after leaving the light on over night. We need to apply this concept and method to OpenVPN or anything really.

Summary

This chapter touched on some of the most common tools used to identify and resolve configuration or network issues within the scope of OpenVPN. Some subjects, such as regular expressions, were identified; however, that may not be obviously useful to a novice administrator.

Some extremely powerful capabilities were also demonstrated with Wireshark's ability to decrypt SSL streams and `tcpdump` able to capture packets. Although these are most useful to an experienced network administrator, they can still be leveraged by a new or novice administrator. Having the ability to extract troubleshooting data is most critical when seeking help from others.

2
Common Problems

There is a fairly consistent theme within the OpenVPN support channels, IRC, the web forums, and the mailing list. The novice users of OpenVPN generally ask the same questions. Most common issues can be resolved by simply dutifully reading the OpenVPN manual (`http://openvpn.net/man`) and taking notes. Although this book aims to inform the reader of additional techniques and tools, the man page is a considerable wealth of knowledge, and the close scrutiny of its contents will be beneficial in the long run.

Based on questions found in IRC and on the forums, the novice OpenVPN administrator struggles most with identifying the root cause of a problem and is generally lost with how to find that cause. The vast majority of problems can be grouped pretty easily into a small subset of issues, often quickly realized with initial configurations:

- Certificate problems
- Incompatible `tun`/`tap` configuration settings between a server and a client
- IP range conflicts with VPN and remote local LAN
- Routing misconceptions
- Incorrect assumptions on utility and layer 4 integration

Outside the common areas mentioned earlier, easily addressed issues, lying just beyond the OpenVPN program influence can confound even the most experienced system administrator. Ensuring that the operating system that the server or client is attempting to use is supported can prevent a configuration from working, right out the gate.

In this chapter, we will cover some of the most common problems associated with OpenVPN server and client implementations. To that end, methods for segregating various components of OpenVPN and identifying and validating those components that are working will be covered. At the end of this chapter, we will prioritize assorted functions, features, and processes to aid in quick problem resolution.

Narrowing the focus

When your VPN fails to work the way it was expected, it's best to narrow down the cause of the problem. In the simplest case, a VPN is used by a client wanting to talk to a resource that exists on the VPN. Having a diagram or flow chart of your finished VPN topology, including the VPN, the server-side LAN, and resources that will be exposed to the clients, will help rule out working components.

Here is a sample network diagram depicting a simple corporate network with an OpenVPN server. There are a number of internal components that are inaccessible to the general Internet, an application server, and an internal website. Externally accessible are a public website, the corporate e-mail server, and the OpenVPN server.

The dotted lines show our protected or internal traffic, and the solid lines show general Internet routed traffic:

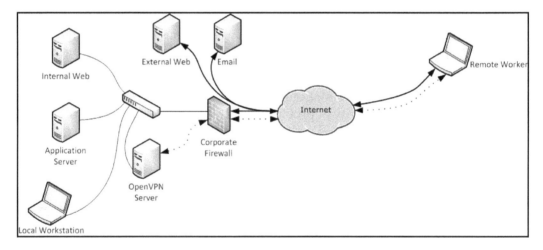

Example network diagram used in scenario 1 and 2

Sample scenarios

The utility of the diagram mentioned earlier are best demonstrated with some useful scenarios. Having the ability to identify a specific component of the network as a potential culprit to a problem, small or large, is important and easiest to understand in a simple, nonproduction case.

In our following scenarios, we have a remote worker, also known as a *road warrior*. These users have historically been sales staff but are increasingly becoming engineers and executives.

Scenario 1–unable to access VPN

The remote worker has reported that she is unable to connect to the VPN. She has stated that the OpenVPN client indicates that she is connected, but she cannot fetch e-mails or see the internal corporate website. Normal web browsing is working. Here are the questions you could ask the user:

- **Does the remote worker have an Internet access?** We can assume so because she has stated that normal web browsing works.
- **Does the client connect to the VPN server?** The remote worker states that the OpenVPN client shows that she is connected to the VPN. This, itself, isn't necessarily telling, as the client can still have routing or other errors that will be more apparent in the logs. The simplest log check is to look for the following in the log on the client or server side:

  2016-04-10 10:11:19 Initialization Sequence Completed

- **Can the remote worker ping the VPN server's internal VPN IP address?** We have omitted IPs within the diagram earlier. The VPN server will have a LAN address as well as a VPN address. Once connected to the VPN, you can look at the `tun` or `tap` device or look in the logs. On Windows, this would be in the normal **Network Connections** control panel; on a Unix system, using `ifconfig` on the correct device is enough, in our case, `utun1`:

```
● ● ●                        author@example
author@example:~--> ifconfig utun1
utun1: flags=8051<UP,POINTOPOINT,RUNNING,MULTICAST> mtu 1500
        inet 192.168.80.2 --> 192.168.80.2 netmask 0xffffff00
author@example:~--> ping -c 4 192.168.80.1
PING 192.168.80.1 (192.168.80.1): 56 data bytes
64 bytes from 192.168.80.1: icmp_seq=0 ttl=64 time=38.060 ms
64 bytes from 192.168.80.1: icmp_seq=1 ttl=64 time=38.601 ms
64 bytes from 192.168.80.1: icmp_seq=2 ttl=64 time=38.349 ms
64 bytes from 192.168.80.1: icmp_seq=3 ttl=64 time=38.397 ms

--- 192.168.80.1 ping statistics ---
4 packets transmitted, 4 packets received, 0.0% packet loss
round-trip min/avg/max/stddev = 38.060/38.352/38.601/0.193 ms
author@example:~--> █
```

Successful ping of VPN server from the client.

We have now validated that the VPN is up and the client is connected. Troubleshooting from here passes to other systems outside the direct control of OpenVPN. There could be a faulty rule in the firewall, or the mail or web server could be offline.

In `Chapter 4`, *The Log File*, we will dig into the log file to ensure all aspects of the configuration were accepted and properly configured. In later chapters, identifying, routing, and other network issues will also be explained. For now, we have passed troubleshooting on to the corporate firewall team because we have verified that actual connectivity to the VPN itself is functional.

Scenario 2–cannot access external web when on VPN

Our hardworking remote worker is finally able to connect to the VPN. Checking e-mails is working great, and all the internal company web resources are available to her. Quickly, however, she realizes that browsing websites not belonging to the company is no longer possible. She has tried some of the common web pages, and checking her personal e-mail account also fails. Another call for support! Here are the questions to ask the user:

- **Does a normal function return after disconnecting?** Having the client side disconnected is useful in isolating the issue to the local LAN. If the problem goes away, there is a good chance that some configuration property is the cause of the issue.
- **Does the issue reoccur once reconnected to the VPN?** Once the VPN connection has been re-established, test that the failure case has returned. If so, we can assign some blame to the VPN as the cause of the issue.
- **What route is the Internet-bound traffic taking?** A common option used by OpenVPN administrators is to route all traffic through the VPN (see the option `--redirect-gateway`).

Take the following diagram into consideration. We have the same corporate network we had earlier, with some external resources, a web server and a personal e-mail server. Without the `--redirect-gateway` option, the traffic flows might resemble the lines in this diagram:

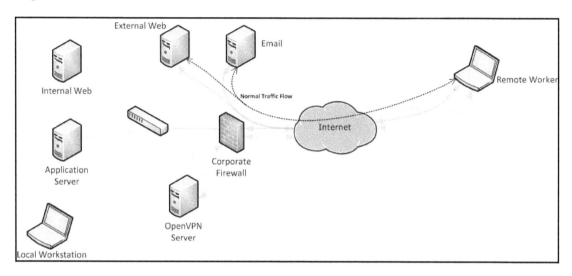

Normal Internet-bound traffic flow

When the `--redirect-gateway` option is added, the the web traffic is also routed through the VPN gateway. Through finer, more specific routing table entries, the VPN effectively overrides the client's default gateway, causing the path of Internet-bound traffic to flow from the client, to the VPN server, and back out to the VPN server's default gateway.

If the gateway isn't configured correctly and the VPN is configured to route all traffic, including Internet-bound traffic, it could be blocked. Some issues could include incorrect **Network Address Translation** (**NAT**) or firewall rules. In this scenario, the LAN resources are functional, but Internet browsing from the client would be dysfunctional.

The following diagram shows traffic passing to the VPN server which is sort of a dead end there. Either the kernel of the operating system doesn't know what to do with it, or traffic is being blocked by a firewall:

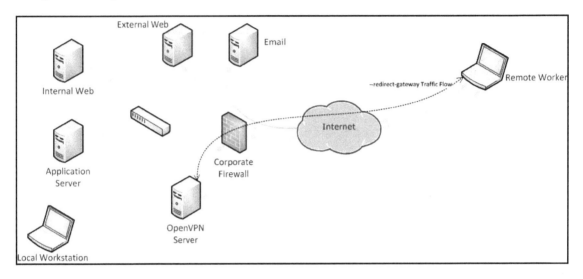

Internet traffic routed to VPN server, blocked at server

If NAT is properly configured, and the firewall rules necessary are defined, a traffic flow should progress from a VPN client to a VPN server, and back out to the Internet. Based on your requirements and configuration, the corporate firewall may come into play, both on inbound and outbound traffic or only on one leg.

Note that the following diagram shows the VPN connection passing through the firewall for both the inbound VPN connection and the outbound Internet traffic. This is subject to the overall network configuration and is demonstrated as a *typical* example. Please don't take this too literally:

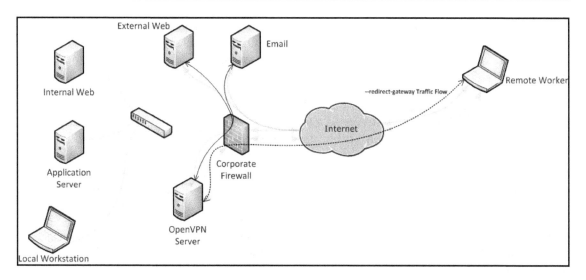

Internet traffic routed to a VPN server: successful flow to Internet

This second scenario was much easier to troubleshoot with the aid of diagrams. Even if you're just creating a VPN for your home network or a quick impromptu VPN at work, a diagram or even a quick sketch will help to identify any problems that may arise.

Network diagrams and flowcharts can be quickly and easily created with a variety of software and tools. Both **Microsoft Visio** and **Gliffy** (https://www.gliffy.com) are paid options; Visio is used for the majority of diagrams in this book. A good free option is **Dia** (http://dia-installer.de).

I attempted to use Gliffy for the diagrams in the book, initially. However, I found that transparency, connection curves, and image setting were much more difficult or unsupported. Overall, it's a good tool, and many of my difficulties were related to some of the constraints I had to overcome authoring this book.

Suspecting recent changes

Once a VPN is up and running successfully, it's a good practice to document the configuration of all aspects. This should include kernel changes such as sysctl, compiled options, network interface values, firewall rules, and routing tables. Having a flow chart of your authentication scheme is also useful.

Any time a change is made to any of the components of the VPN, be sure to update your documentation and keep copies of the old versions. Quite often, a seemingly innocuous change will prove to be the culprit when there is a later failure. Solid documentation will aid in identifying what, specifically, changes from your working state to your non-working state.

One specific example from IRC involved a long time idler who is relatively knowledgeable with OpenVPN and routinely helps other users. This user had a working OpenVPN setup with **Amazon Web Services** (**AWS**) and switched to another provider, but both companies provided Red Hat 6 VMs. The existing configuration files, certificate, and key would be copied to the new host. The *only* change was to be the external IP address of the new VM.

I worked with this user for hours over the course of a few days analyzing firewall rules, configuration, network settings, to no avail. Finally, another user was following our dialogue and poked at the new provider's website and chimed in, *Oh, they use OpenVZ. Did they grant your VM tun/tap access?*

Sure enough, the user was able to log in to the support portal to request the device access and the VPN started working.

Supported operating systems

Arguably, the easiest thing to resolve is identifying an operating system that has proper support for OpenVPN. If the `tun` or `tap` device is not supported, it quickly rules out OpenVPN or limits the specific features of OpenVPN, but is often overlooked. Both iOS (all versions as of this writing) and Android (also, all versions as of this writing) do not support the `tap` device.

There are other operating systems that don't support virtualized network devices at all. FreeBSD jails, for example, don't support the `tun` or `tap` devices without some significant configuration and startup tricks. Many embedded operating systems, generally on routers and switches, do not fully support OpenVPN. Even if your platform of choice claims to support the virtual network devices, it's best to do some digging to ensure that OpenVPN runs reliably.

Embedded devices

There is a long list of embedded devices that support OpenVPN. Snom VOIP phones have the ability to support OpenVPN for secure telephony (`http://wiki.snom.com/Networking/Virtual_Private_Network_(VPN)`) using a custom firmware available on the Snom website. Some **off-the-shelf** (**OTS**) home routers, such as Asus RT-AC5300, support OpenVPN right out of the box:

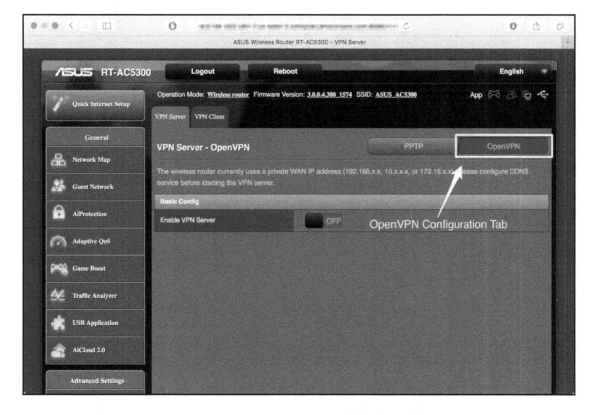

Many other router firmware packages support OpenVPN. **OpenWrt** (`https://openwrt.org`), **DD-WRT** (`http://www.dd-wrt.com/site/index`), and **Tomato Firmware** (`http://www.polarcloud.com/tomato`) are likely the most commonly known. These firmware packages fully support OpenVPN and, most importantly, the required virtual networking devices.

When evaluating an embedded firmware or platform, make certain that it supports either the `tap` or `tun` virtual network devices. The latter is most important, as (you'll find out later) it is the most common, and correct, device to use. Without one or the other, you can safely rule out OS.

Most of these systems provide a web interface to help configure the OpenVPN server, often with a limited feature set. The disadvantage with these is that some advanced features are either missing entirely or confusing to set up. For the best troubleshooting and configuration experience, I recommend you to find some way to access the underlying text configuration or at a minimum, the command-line arguments passed on execution.

OpenVPN is a unique protocol in a family of SSL-based VPNs. OpenVPN will not work with other protocols including other SSL VPNs, such as Cisco's **AnyConnect** or non-SSL-based VPN protocols such as **IPSec**, **Point-to-Point Tunneling Protocol** (**PPTP**), or others.

Semi-embedded systems

There is a class of systems that I have termed *semi-embedded*. These systems run a *firmware* that resides on a relatively normal PC or computer system, but is highly tailored to a specific use. A couple of these systems including **FreeNAS** (http://freenas.org), an open source network filer, and **pfSense** (http://pfsense.org), an open source firewall and network gateway device, have OpenVPN plugins or modules. Some additional systems that support OpenVPN in this category, both open source and closed, are:

- **ReadyNAS** (via external package): http://readynas.com
- **TrueNAS** (based on FreeNAS, similar packages work): https://www.ixsystems.com/truenas/
- **Synolgoy**: https://www.synology.com/en-us/
- **QNAP**: https://www.qnap.com/

At the time of writing this, these systems support OpenVPN. It's important to note that these systems can pull or remove support at any time, and may not support OpenVPN in specific use case scenarios (lack of support for `tap` is common).

An administrator should evaluate if their use, either with a private network, or with a particular version of firmware, supports the use of the correct virtual adapter or OpenVPN software package.

The **Transport Layer Security** (**TLS**) list of supported ciphers will vary on these embedded devices as well. Ciphers using **Advanced Encryption Standard** (**AES**) may perform well on desktop systems, but will show a performance bottleneck over other ciphers on some embedded systems. Most modern processors support **AES New Instruction** (**AES-NI**), which offloads AES calculations to a subprocessor specifically designed for that workload. Embedded systems tend to be low power and purpose built, so are likely to lack this feature. Cipher differences will be further discussed in Chapter 8, *Performance*.

Virtual servers

Virtual private servers (**VPSs**) are likely the most common point of pain for an aspiring OpenVPN administrator. Particularly with Linux, there is a plethora of environments in which a Linux system can be deployed virtually including **Kernel-based Virtual Machine** (**KVM**), **Quick EMUlator** (**QEMU**), and **OpenVZ** (Virtuozzo Containers).

OpenVZ is particularly difficult to configure. When VPS is purchased from a larger provider, cooperation is required from that provider. With OpenVZ, the container needs to be specifically granted access to the `tun` and `tap` adapters. With FreeBSD jails, the routing of VPN traffic actually takes place outside the jail in the host kernel.

 OpenVZ is a very popular virtualization technology for Linux with various hosting providers. The OpenVZ wiki has a good write-up on working with OpenVPN and the changes needed to make it work at `http ://wiki.openvz.org/VPN_via_the_TUN/TAP_device`.

IP addresses

It is important to choose an IP address range that does not have or has goods odds against, conflicting with remote client address pools. If VPN uses IP addresses from a range shared by a remote client address pool, packets meant for the client LAN may attempt to traverse the VPN to the wrong system or to a system that doesn't exist at all. Alternatively, the traffic may never leave the client LAN and be routed to a local resource, instead.

The following diagram illustrates a fairly severe case of what I'm describing. There are various resources identified with their associated LAN address on both sides.

On the left, there is a network where the VPN server resides. The LAN on the server network uses the `10.4.0.0/24` subnet. For the VPN, the `10.8.0.0/24` subnet is used. This will facilitate VPN traffic, and a route will be pushed for the server-side LAN subnet. There are two internal servers for which the VPN was created. The first is an application server using LAN IP `10.4.0.76` and an internal web server using IP `10.4.0.33`.

On the right side of the diagram, we show the client network. The client network also uses the `10.4.0.0/24` subnet. A laptop is on the network with a VPN address of `10.0.8.6` and a LAN address of `10.4.0.76`. There is also a local printer with IP `10.4.0.33`:

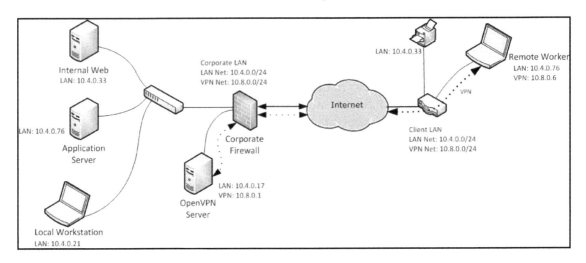

Network diagram showing IP conflicts between network segments

There are quite a few problems with this setup. Generally, these can all be resolved by changing one IP range or the other. If the VPN server pushes a route for the `10.4.0.0/24` subnet, the remote client will lose its connection to all local resources, such as the printer, but also it's a default gateway. Once the default gateway is overridden, the client will drop the VPN connection, beginning a vicious cycle of connecting, dropping, and reconnecting.

If the VPN server, instead, pushes the `--redirect-gateway` directive with `def 1` arguments, then the client's local LAN and Internet routing will be overridden, but the default gateway of the LAN will be preserved. This prevents the reconnect cycle, but will render the local printer unusable.

Another solution would be to translate all of the corporate resource to VPN range IPs. It involves creating a mapping from a VPN address to the remote corporate LAN address. This allows the VPN clients to use VPN addresses for all remote services, negating problems with IP conflict.

Using OpenBSD's pf syntax, all of the corporate resources have been NATed to VPN IPs here:

```
# PF NAT rules for corporate resources
int_web =   10.4.0.33
int_app =   10.4.0.76
vpn_web =   10.8.0.200
vpn_app =   10.8.0.201
pass on eth0 from $int_web to any binat-to $vpn_web
pass on eth0 from $int_app to any binat-to $vpn_app
```

 While I prefer the OpenBSD packet filter, many users will be most familiar with the Linux **iptables**. Karl Rupp has a detailed write-up of iptables on Linux relating to NAT. Rather than rehashing his content, check it out at http://www.karlrupp.net/en/computer/nat_tutorial!

Additional work would be needed for the solution to fully function. Pushing custom DNS servers with VPN-specific DNS views would allow VPN clients to resolve http://internal.example.org to 10.8.0.200 instead of the normal 10.4.0.33, for example. The NAT rules allow the traffic to flow from the VPN to the internal corporate network without having to push the corporate network subnet to the VPN clients.

Fortunately, there are a lot of options out there. The **Internet Engineering Task Force (IETF)** at http://ietf.org has defined a **Request For Comments (RFC)**, RFC 1918 (https://www.ietf.org/rfc/rfc1918.txt). For IPv4, this RFC clearly defines the IP ranges that should be used for private network subnets, and there is a relatively large set of subnets defined:

- 10.0.0.0 – 10.255.255.255 (10/8 prefix)
- 192.168.0.0 – 192.168.255.255 (192.168/16 prefix)
- 172.16.0.0 – 172.31.255.255 (172.16/12 prefix)

Of the preceding three groups, there has been a trend in utilization that can be easily worked around in individual deployments. This is not a hard and fast rule or regulation. Any network administrator can define whatever subnets they chose:

- 10.0.0.0: Used primarily on large corporate networks for the LAN.
- 192.168.0.0: Home and consumer routers, specifically 192.168.0.0/24 and 192.168.1.0/24. The remainder of the /16 is up for grabs!
- 172.16.0.0: Corporations typically use this for DMZs and VPN subnet ranges.

If we convert our client-side LAN range to the common `192.168.0.0/24` subnet, we find a very different traffic path. Both servers on the VPN side have a clear route and path from the client:

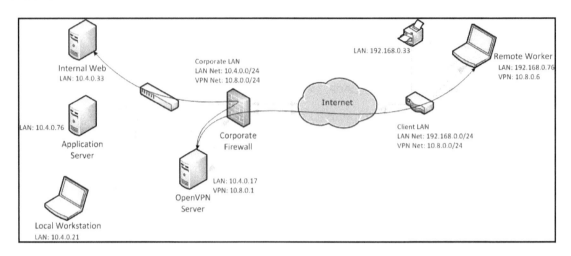

 There is a similar RFC for IPv6 private address ranges, RFC 4193. You can read more details about it on the IETF website: `https://tools.ietf.org/html/rfc4193`

The OpenVPN *HOWTO* (`https://openvpn.net/howto`) uses the `10.8.0.0/24` network in the examples presented. This is a somewhat random subnet within the 10/8 class-a subnet, but there is a chance, with large corporations, that this will conflict.

There is an even better chance, however, that this will remain unused for most home users. Ensure that your VPN IP range selection is thought out and properly engineered with regard to the likely client networks, and the known server-side network.

Setting up a VPN at home, it is recommended to avoid the `192.168.0.0/24` and `192.168.1.0/24` subnet ranges. These two are most common on home routers as the default. While it will work fine from remote offices, connecting from other routers with these default configurations will result in conflicting address space.

Many corporate networks use `10.0.0.0/8` or some subnets within that range. For this reason, it is also a good idea to avoid these addresses. It seems to be common to use `172.16.0.0/12` for VPNs and DMZs in corporate environments, so it's likely safe to use this range for your own VPN as well.

Firewalls

Incorrectly configured firewalls are one of the most prevalent problem areas, particularly for new users. Experienced users are also apt for misunderstanding how firewall rules apply to OpenVPN routed packets. In the past, firewalls were relatively monolithic devices at or near a network edge. Today, however, firewalls exist on client devices, network devices, all along the path of a network packet. Any switch in the path can have ACLs preventing or permitting traffic. This can include both the client- and server-side LANs. The OpenVPN likely has a firewall element for translation or routing traffic, and also for preventing or permitting said traffic.

The monolithic firewall also still exists and can be a pain point when troubleshooting traffic flow. The current high-end firewalls also permit deep packet inspection, SSL decryption, and what some vendors term *zero-day patching*. The latter generally requires SSL decryption be configured and permits the firewall vendor to detect vulnerable applications or protocols and modify the traffic real time. In my experience with both Palo Alto Networks and Sophos products, OpenVPN will not function through these decryption profiles.

 The SSL decryption capabilities will generally work fine for normal web browsing traffic, but other applications that use TLS will break when they pass through such a firewall with this feature enabled. Apart from OpenVPN, both Bomgar and Dell KACE are also functionally broken when passing through one of the firewalls.

The simplest method for troubleshooting firewall rules is to disable filtering for your VPN traffic and work to re-enable rules until the problem filter has been identified.

Duplicate client certificates

By default, OpenVPN expects each remote client to connect using a unique certificate for identification and encryption purposes. The **common name** (**CN**), is used to generate configuration options, identify a persistent IP (`--ifconfig-pool-persist`), and CCD (`--client-config-dir`) entries. In addition, startup scripts may use the CN to generate dynamic routes, firewall rules, and other access policies.

For the majority of general road-warriors, special routing, and firewall rules are not the norm. In this scenario, the user connects to the VPN, is given an IP address from the server, and they will then have access to the resources of the corporate network. More advanced configurations may provide differing pushed routes or IP assignments in varying subnets.

Overcomplication

It is important to have the intended use of your VPN well defined before starting your troubleshooting endeavors. Understanding how the system is meant to be accessed and used will rule out unrelated problems quickly. I have encountered a plethora of aspiring administrators with gross misconceptions for how OpenVPN should behave, who are pulling their hair out in frustration.

You might want to start simple and get a basic VPN operational before rolling in all the custom routes, authentication mechanisms, reporting, and so on. Following a simple how to and reading the man pages will get you off on the right foot.

Break up complicated configurations into smaller components when attempting to identify the root cause of a failure. Analyze general network settings and deployed configurations first, then move on to more complex components. Assigning static IPs, client-specific configuration components, and firewall rules can come second. As you progress through your setup and verify that a given element is functioning as desired, add it back in to the mix.

Summary

Some of the most common configuration and deployment scenarios were covered in this chapter. In addition to identifying specific potential problems, we've demonstrated how to properly document your OpenVPN network and use diagrams for easier troubleshooting once problems occur. Preferably, identify the entire installation base and your configuration components prior to publishing your VPN to your customers or clients.

We have also helped to identify firewalls, IP address ranges, and operating system incompatibilities as potential problem areas.

3
Installing OpenVPN

There is a multitude of clients available to connect to an OpenVPN server. This chapter helps the administrator troubleshoot client installation errors. We will cover both the open source clients as well as a few commercial alternatives. This chapter will cover these topics and help the administrator resolve common problems.

Common installation problems

OpenVPN installation problems can be classified into a few major categories: adapter or driver problems, lack of necessary permissions, and broken installers. It is also possible that the existing packages for your chosen operating system either do not exist or are greatly out of date.

Compiling OpenVPN

On Linux and Unix systems, compiling from source can sometimes be the only way to get OpenVPN installed. There are packages available for the majority of operating system releases, but there are custom systems (Raspberry Pi, BeagleBone, OpenWrt, and so on) that may not have the latest version of OpenVPN available. Given a proper development environment, the OpenVPN installation should be pretty straightforward.

The required development environment basically consists of the following software components:

- `autoconf` (http://www.gnu.org/software/autoconf/)
- `automake` (http://www.gnu.org/software/automake/)
- C code compilers, such as `gcc`, `clang`, `msvc`, and `cc`, should all work

To demonstrate a software built on a nontypical system, we will compile the OpenVPN 2.3.11 source code on Raspbian, which is a Debian distribution compiled for the Raspberry Pi. In our case, we're using Raspberry Pi B+.

First, download the source code. Links for downloading can be found on the OpenVPN community web page at https://openvpn.net/index.php/open-source/downloads.html. Once downloaded, extract the GZIP-compressed .tar file:

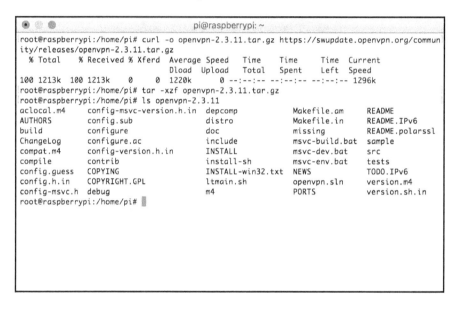

OpenVPN source download and extraction

Before open source software packaging was so common, software was downloaded in source form. To install these software distributions, it needed to be compiled. Tools like those mentioned earlier (autoconf and automake) made this process much easier by breaking the process down into the three steps, namely using configure, make, and make install.

However, in the case of our Raspbian OpenVPN installation, we discover that the ./configure step fails due to missing SSL libraries (see the second to the last line of output in the screenshot here):

```
●  ●  ●                                  pi@raspberrypi: ~
checking for net/if_tun.h... no
checking net/tun/if_tun.h usability... no
checking net/tun/if_tun.h presence... no
checking for net/tun/if_tun.h... no
checking linux/if_tun.h usability... yes
checking linux/if_tun.h presence... yes
checking for linux/if_tun.h... yes
checking tap-windows.h usability... no
checking tap-windows.h presence... no
checking for tap-windows.h... no
checking whether TUNSETPERSIST is declared... yes
checking for setcon in -lselinux... no
checking for pam_start in -lpam... no
checking for PKCS11_HELPER... no
checking for OPENSSL_CRYPTO... no
checking for RSA_new in -lcrypto... no
checking for OPENSSL_SSL... no
checking for SSL_CTX_new in -lssl... no
checking for ssl_init in -lpolarssl... no
checking for aes_crypt_cbc in -lpolarssl... no
checking for lzo1x_1_15_compress in -llzo2... no
checking for lzo1x_1_15_compress in -llzo... no
checking git checkout... no
configure: error:  ssl is required but missing
root@raspberrypi:/home/pi/openvpn-2.3.11#
```

/configure failure at the end – ssl libraries are missing

OpenSSL has been the *de facto* standard of SSL libraries for quite a few years, but a relative new comer is also supported by OpenVPN: **mbed TLS**.

Here, we back up one directory, download the mbed TLS source package, extract, and compile. A simple `make` command is all that is needed to build mbed TLS once the software is extracted. Note that running `compile` on a small embedded system such as Raspberry Pi will take considerably longer than it would on a more robust desktop or server system. In our test case, the mbed TLS (**PolarSSL**) `make` process took approximately 20 minutes.

 PolarSSL changed their name to mbed TLS in 2016 when ARM acquired the project. OpenVPN 2.3.11 and earlier need to use the older 1.3.x libraries, which are still named PolarSSL. The name and references were changed in 2.3.12 and later (2.3-master, as of this writing).

```
● ● ●                          pi@raspberrypi: ~
root@raspberrypi:/home/pi/openvpn-2.3.11# cd ..
root@raspberrypi:/home/pi# curl -o polarssl-1.3.9.tgz  https://tls.mbed.org/download/polarss
l-1.3.9-gpl.tgz
  % Total    % Received % Xferd  Average Speed   Time    Time     Time  Current
                                 Dload  Upload   Total   Spent    Left  Speed
100 1700k  100 1700k    0     0    273k     0  0:00:06  0:00:06 --:--:--  364k
root@raspberrypi:/home/pi# tar -xzf polarssl-1.3.9.tgz
root@raspberrypi:/home/pi# cd polarssl-1.3.9
root@raspberrypi:/home/pi/polarssl-1.3.9# ls
ChangeLog       configs               doxygen  library  Makefile  README.rst  tests
CMakeLists.txt  DartConfiguration.tcl  include  LICENSE  programs  scripts     visualc
root@raspberrypi:/home/pi/polarssl-1.3.9# make
  CC    aes.c
  CC    aesni.c
```

Download and extraction of the mbed TLS software bundle

The default SSL library for OpenVPN is OpenSSL, so using mbed TLS requires an option for `configure`. Note the `configure` command in the associated option in the following screenshot. For a full list of `configure` options, run `configure` with `--help`:

```
● ● ●                          pi@raspberrypi: ~
configure: creating ./config.status
config.status: creating version.sh
config.status: creating Makefile
config.status: creating build/Makefile
config.status: creating build/msvc/Makefile
config.status: creating build/msvc/msvc-generate/Makefile
config.status: creating distro/Makefile
config.status: creating distro/rpm/Makefile
config.status: creating distro/rpm/openvpn.spec
config.status: creating include/Makefile
config.status: creating src/Makefile
config.status: creating src/compat/Makefile
config.status: creating src/openvpn/Makefile
config.status: creating src/openvpnserv/Makefile
config.status: creating src/plugins/Makefile
config.status: creating src/plugins/auth-pam/Makefile
config.status: creating src/plugins/down-root/Makefile
config.status: creating tests/Makefile
config.status: creating sample/Makefile
config.status: creating doc/Makefile
config.status: creating tests/t_client.sh
config.status: creating config.h
config.status: executing depfiles commands
config.status: executing libtool commands
root@raspberrypi:/home/pi/openvpn-2.3.11#
```

The configuration is complete without additional errors

After installing the PolarSSL libraries, I needed to *export* two environment variables, LDFLAGS and CFLAGS, to tell configure where to find the new libraries. Once done, I was able to successfully complete the configure operation:

```
root@raspberrypi:/home/pi/openvpn-2.3.11# export CFLAGS=
-I/home/pi/polarssl-1.3.9/include root@raspberrypi:/home/pi/
openvpn-2.3.11# export LDFLAGS=-L/home/pi/polarssl-1.3.9/library
root@raspberrypi:/home/pi/openvpn-2.3.11# ./configure --with-crypto
-library=polarssl --disable-lzo
```

Two additional libraries missing were found on our Raspbian installation besides the SSL libraries. We opted to disable the LZO compression algorithm for expediency, but needed to install the libpam-dev package using apt-get:

```
# apt-get install libpam-dev
```

Now that the build environment has been configured, thanks to autoconf, the OpenVPN software can be compiled and installed. It is easiest to do this in a single command operation:

```
root@raspberrypi:/home/pi/openvpn-2.3.11# make && make install
```

The final screenshot in this section shows a successful software-build and installation. The which Unix command shows that the openvpn binary has been installed in /usr/local/bin/. Running openvpn with the --version option shows the build date, compile time options, and supporting libraries.

Most notably, we've built OpenVPN with the PolarSSL 1.3.9 libraries on ARM:

```
pi@raspberrypi: ~
/usr/bin/install -c -m 644 README README.IPv6 README.polarssl COPYRIGHT.GPL COPYING '/usr/l
ocal/share/doc/openvpn'
make[3]: Leaving directory '/home/pi/openvpn-2.3.11'
make[2]: Leaving directory '/home/pi/openvpn-2.3.11'
make[1]: Leaving directory '/home/pi/openvpn-2.3.11'
root@raspberrypi:/home/pi/openvpn-2.3.11# which openvpn
/usr/local/sbin/openvpn
root@raspberrypi:/home/pi/openvpn-2.3.11# openvpn --version
OpenVPN 2.3.11 armv6l-unknown-linux-gnueabihf [SSL (PolarSSL)] [EPOLL] [MH] [IPv6] built on
Jun 29 2016
library versions: PolarSSL 1.3.9
Originally developed by James Yonan
Copyright (C) 2002-2010 OpenVPN Technologies, Inc. <sales@openvpn.net>
Compile time defines: enable_crypto=yes enable_crypto_ofb_cfb=yes enable_debug=yes enable_de
f_auth=yes enable_dlopen=unknown enable_dlopen_self=unknown enable_dlopen_self_static=unknow
n enable_fast_install=yes enable_fragment=yes enable_http_proxy=yes enable_iproute2=no enabl
e_libtool_lock=yes enable_lzo=no enable_lzo_stub=no enable_management=yes enable_multi=yes e
nable_multihome=yes enable_pam_dlopen=no enable_pedantic=no enable_pf=yes enable_pkcs11=no e
nable_plugin_auth_pam=yes enable_plugin_down_root=yes enable_plugins=yes enable_port_share=y
es enable_selinux=no enable_server=yes enable_shared=yes enable_shared_with_static_runtimes=
no enable_small=no enable_socks=yes enable_ssl=yes enable_static=yes enable_strict=no enable
_strict_options=no enable_systemd=no enable_win32_dll=yes enable_x509_alt_username=no with_a
ix_soname=aix with_crypto_library=polarssl with_gnu_ld=yes with_mem_check=no with_plugindir=
'$(libdir)/openvpn/plugins' with_sysroot=no
root@raspberrypi:/home/pi/openvpn-2.3.11#
```

Successful build. OpenVPN 2.3.11 with PolarSSL 1.3.9 built on June 29, 2016 on ARM architecture

Packages and installers

The OpenVPN project members release and maintain a few operating system packages directly, namely Windows, Debian, Ubuntu, and FreeBSD. All other packages or installers are generated and maintained by third-party developers, not generally associated with the OpenVPN development team.

Build-errors do occur, even with the official installers and software packages. These generally occur when changes are made to the project-build structure and are quickly identified by the developers or reported by users. A fix for such issues is usually published within a couple of days or less.

The advantage of the official packages is that the developers of OpenVPN are responsible for the installers. They will know about `configure` and `build` option changes, so they will be able to adjust the package build accordingly. In addition, the common support flow from end users will go to the OpenVPN developers first, who can then make the corrections.

When the installer or package is not directly maintained by an OpenVPN developer, the flow of support can be a bit disjointed from the user base. As mentioned earlier, the users of OpenVPN will first reach out to the developer team when an issue is identified. Whether it be via IRC, the e-mail list, or the forums, correcting the broken component may not be possible due to the lack of repository access or unfamiliarity with the given distribution's packaging methods or policies. The general advice with these situations is to contact the package maintainer directly. This isn't to say third-party packages are bad, but there are just extra steps required when the support is needed.

Linux and other OS distributions will test their packages or installers prior to release. It's usually a safe assumption that these released versions will be functional. The primary complaint seen in the support channels is about out of date software packages. The OpenVPN project covers a wide swathe of different operating systems, which leaves some less common ones to fend for their own installers. In these cases, our suggestion is to simply build from source.

The advantages of precompiled installers

There are a few notable advantages of using precompiled installers or packages. The key advantage is the startup and shutdown routines. OpenVPN, for the near future, will be capable of starting with a fairly simple command line akin to the screenshot here, even on Windows, which is notoriously graphical-interface centric:

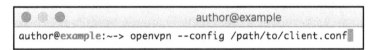

The command-line example of OpenVPN startup using a configuration file

This startup meets the most basic needs, but does not integrate well with modern operating systems. The upcoming 2.4 OpenVPN release is purported to support an OpenVPN service that would allow non-administrators to start OpenVPN sessions without escalating privileges. This would be a multifaceted approach to loading a daemon, and interfacing with that daemon, including authentication and authorization, and triggering the startup of a given profile. This is far more complex than the simple command-line example.

Red Hat Linux (and others) are supporting a centralized system control daemon known as `systemd`. With `systemd`, a unit file defines a service, and `systemd` will start or stop a given service based on the properties within the service's unit file.

The added complication of these newer mechanisms makes the bar to entry much higher, resulting in an increased likelihood of errors and failed startup or shutdown. While newer and more complex, if you stick to the OS-distributed release, these complexities will be handled for you. Deviating from that release to the base source distribution may result in some headache. The disadvantage is many OS package releases lag behind the project release cycle, sometimes, by a month or longer.

Driver installation

OpenVPN uses virtual network adapters to create point-to-point tunnels with remote systems. The `tun` and `tap` adapters are used, based on what type of network traffic is required to flow across the network. Layer 2 (data link) traffic in the OSI model requires the `tap` adapter. This is useful for various routing protocols and applications or games that depend on broadcast traffic. More commonly, layer 3 (network) traffic is all that is required, which uses the `tun` adapter.

 Further details about the **Open Systems Interconnection** (**OSI**) model can be found at Wikipedia (`https://en.wikipedia.org/wiki/OSI_model`) or the International Organization for Standardization (`http://standards.iso.org/ittf/PubliclyAvailableStandards/s02026 9_ISO_IEC_7498-1_1994(E).zip`) websites.

On the majority of Linux and Unix platforms, there will be two distinct virtual network adapters, `tun` and `tap`. Linux aliases the bridging Ethernet pseudo adapter to `tap` and `bond`, with a distinct `tun` kernel module. FreeBSD, on the other hand, includes both the `tun` and `tap` functionality in the `if_tap.ko` kernel module.

On Windows, the OpenVPN project provides the **TAP-Windows** virtual network adapter. The OpenVPN GUI installer will normally install the driver for you, but the installer is available separately. The driver is available in two forms: NDIS 5 (TAP-Windows, version 9.9.x) for Windows XP and NDIS 6 (TAP-Windows6, 9.21.x) for Windows Vista and higher.

If more than a single OpenVPN instance will be running at once, an additional TAP-Windows adapter device will need to be installed. Fortunately, OpenVPN provides the tools needed to create additional interfaces. There are two distinct methods to install additional virtual network adapters:

- The `tapinstall.exe` utility
- The Control Panel new hardware wizard

The first method involves using the `tapinstall.exe` utility provided with current versions of OpenVPN. The binary can be found in `C:\Program Files\TAP-Windows\bin`. This tool can be used to query what adapters are currently installed, as well as adding or removing devices:

```
C:\Program Files\TAP-Windows\bin>..\..\OpenVPN\bin\openvpn.exe --show-adapters
Available TAP-WIN32 adapters [name, GUID]:
'Local Area Connection 2' {2878976F-EAD0-4F7F-BF26-6ADB609C519A}

C:\Program Files\TAP-Windows\bin>tapinstall.exe hwids tap*
ROOT\NET\0001
    Name: TAP-Windows Adapter V9
    Hardware IDs:
        tap0901
1 matching device(s) found.

C:\Program Files\TAP-Windows\bin>tapinstall.exe install ..\driver\OemVista.inf tap0901
Device node created. Install is complete when drivers are installed...
Updating drivers for tap0901 from C:\Program Files\TAP-Windows\driver\OemVista.inf.
Drivers installed successfully.

C:\Program Files\TAP-Windows\bin>tapinstall.exe hwids tap*
ROOT\NET\0005
    Name: TAP-Windows Adapter V9 #2
    Hardware IDs:
        tap0901
ROOT\NET\0001
    Name: TAP-Windows Adapter V9
    Hardware IDs:
        tap0901
2 matching device(s) found.

C:\Program Files\TAP-Windows\bin>tapinstall.exe remove tap0901
ROOT\NET\0005                                              : Removed
ROOT\NET\0001                                              : Removed
2 device(s) were removed.

C:\Program Files\TAP-Windows\bin>tapinstall.exe hwids tap*
No matching devices found.

C:\Program Files\TAP-Windows\bin>tapinstall.exe install ..\driver\OemVista.inf tap0901
Device node created. Install is complete when drivers are installed...
Updating drivers for tap0901 from C:\Program Files\TAP-Windows\driver\OemVista.inf.
Drivers installed successfully.

C:\Program Files\TAP-Windows\bin>tapinstall.exe hwids foo*
ROOT\NET\0004
    Hardware IDs:
        foo
1 matching device(s) found.

C:\Program Files\TAP-Windows\bin>
```

The preceding screenshot shows a full cycle using the utility, displaying the list of adapters (just one), installing an additional adapter, removing all adapters, and reinstalling a new adapter. More information about the tool can be found with the `/?` command-line option or by going to the TAP-Windows adapter wiki page at `https://community.openvpn.net/ope nvpn/wiki/ManagingWindowsTAPDrivers`.

The device drivers for the TAP-Windows adapter reside in the `C:\Program Files\TAP-Windows\driver` directory. This is where you should point the new hardware wizard when attempting option two, mentioned earlier.

I recommend using this second method, particularly, if you are not comfortable on the Windows command line. Also, the `tapinstall.exe` utility is fairly indiscriminate when removing the adapter: it's all or nothing. The **Device Manager** option easily allows you to add or remove specific adapters. This becomes more important once you become dependent on specifically named adapters for more complex routing scenarios.

Alternative clients

From an open source project perspective, the only supported application is a build of the open source project code. In practice, however, there are a multitude of exceedingly useful alternative builds. Some of these builds are for commercial VPN providers, and support not just the OpenVPN protocol, but may include support for PPTP, IPSec, or AnyConnect, or any other protocol. These applications usually provide a single, simple, user interface, and couple with a custom configuration provided by the author or provider.

Because of the added features or controls that may be built into the third-party application, it's likely easiest to troubleshoot a non-working OpenVPN connection by reverting back to the open source client. This helps to rule out the additional features.

There are a few circumstances where an official application does not exactly exist. Mobile platforms, for instance, do not have a native OpenVPN open source build. The Android OpenVPN client, while using the majority of the OpenVPN base source, still requires a frontend GUI to manipulate the connection.

There is an application (OpenVPN Connect), provided by the commercial venture of James Yonan, but that currently uses a large amount of experimental and out-of-band source that isn't shared with the community. James has put in quite a bit of effort to make it compatible, but there are known limitations and certain incompatibilities between the commercial application and other applications.

Summary

In this chapter, we discussed how OpenVPN is installed and compiled, including some of the benefits of using software packages distributed by your operating system of choice. There are many places where a compilation or installation of OpenVPN can turn sour, and being cognizant of those will help you create a successful and maintainable VPN.

I think the hardest market today is the mobile market, primarily due to the lockdown of some application marketplaces and the restrictions placed on the environment and ecosystem. Being aware of these as well as some of the limitations of a given platform should set up correct and workable expectations.

In the next chapter, we dig into the log file, helping you identify problems and recognize some of the solutions indicated in the log messages. The previous chapters primarily covered the bases of how OpenVPN functions, how it's built, but only works on functional setups.

4
The Log File

Logs become irreplaceable resources when problems arise in almost anything. Meeting notes, registration sheets, visitor comment cards, and Syslog entries are all signs of logs that can be used to track down problem trends and identify troublesome changes that may have occurred.

OpenVPN has a multitude of logging capabilities that allow the system administrators to track active connections, session setup and negotiation, authentication, and more. In addition, the level of verbosity can be adjusted by making the logs more useful during changes and reducing disk consumption when the VPN is stable.

This chapter will describe the various logging options in OpenVPN. The ability to mute repetitive log entries, build responsive logging and usage interfaces, and tune the logs for the state of the VPN, such as recent changes, new features, or problematic clients, are all possible with well-tuned configuration options.

Logging options

The best source of information when troubleshooting OpenVPN connection and configuration problems is the log file, whether it is on the server or the client. OpenVPN provides a multitude of logging options, allowing an administrator to best gather the data necessary to resolve a problem. This book may be the first comprehensive guide to what is logged by OpenVPN and how best to respond to the messages in that log.

In order to successfully tune the logging of your OpenVPN client or server, it's important to understand what the available logging options are and what impact they will have on the available troubleshooting data. This section will provide a detailed description of every logging option found in the 2.3.11 release of OpenVPN. The following command defines the file where log data will be written out:

```
--log file
```

It is suggested the entire path be included, but if `--cd` is used, or when applying the option from the command line, it's reasonable to use a relative path instead. It should be noted that if the file already exists, it will be truncated upon startup. If the file does not exist, it will be created, assuming the user executing the process has sufficient permissions.

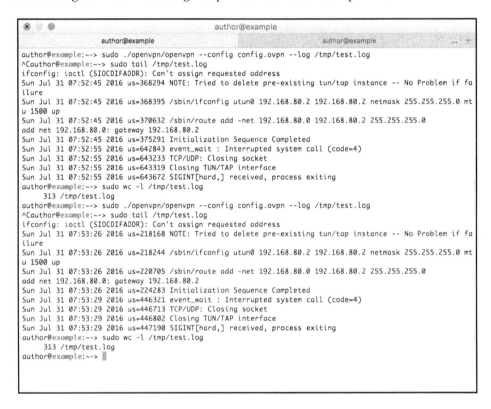

Demonstrating –log and the log file truncate behavior

In the preceding screenshot, we ran a simple OpenVPN connection in the active terminal tab. We monitored the `/tmp/test.log` file in the inactive tab for connection initialization, so we would know when we could press *Ctrl + C* and terminate the session.

Here, you can see that messages are properly written to `/tmp/test.log` and upon closing, that log has 313 lines. When we rerun the connection, the log is truncated and the second connection results in 313 lines written to the file. The `--log-append` option works nearly identically to the `--log` option, except that the file, if it already exists, will be appended to, rather than truncated:

```
--log-append file
```

If you are writing to a log file, it is suggested that you use this option:

Demonstrating–log-append no longer truncates the log

In the previous screenshot, `--log-append` is used on the command line instead of `--log` (`verb 4` is present within the testing configuration file). We removed the previous log file to avoid confusion and demonstrate that the log file is created and, like before, we have 313 lines in the log after a successful connect and disconnect cycle.

We run the connection a second time, and we are left with 627 lines in the log. Both execution logs now remain. We noted that 627 is not the same as 313 x 2, so we dug into the log and discovered that our second execution resulted in a repeated `PUSH_REQUEST`, likely due to a packet retransmission.

When using the `--daemon` option, and lacking any `--log` or `--log-append` option, output will be redirected to the default Syslog file. Any of the other log options will supersede the `--daemon` option's Syslog call:

```
--daemon [program_name]
```

If the `[program_name]` option is specified, `program_name` will be prepended to all Syslog lines related to OpenVPN. If you have multiple OpenVPN instances on a single system or you send your Syslog entries to a remote system, the `[program_name]` option may help differentiate between the various instances:

Syslog output with program_name defined

Much like the `--daemon` option, the `--syslog` option allows us to send logs to the system Syslog:

`--syslog [program_name]`

This option is redundant when using `--daemon`, but becomes useful when running OpenVPN on the command line while still allowing logs to be directed to the system logging daemon. As with `--daemon`, the other logging directives will override the `--syslog` option.

The `--verb` option has a great impact on logging usefulness when it comes to troubleshooting:

`--verb n`

Set correctly, a working VPN can confirm correct functionality with confidence, while also presenting useful information when a VPN experiences issues.

The higher the number passed to this directive (`[n]`), the more verbose the logging. The next section, *Logging levels*, goes further in depth and provides the examples of both working logs as well as some logs with errors.

The following option prevents OpenVPN from prepending timestamps to the output log lines:

`--suppress-timestamps`

I suggest this option not be used as it makes pinpointing where and when a problem actually occurred.

The `--mute` directive prevents OpenVPN from repeating more than `[n]` log messages of the same mute category:

`--mute [n]`

The mute category of a log entry does not directly follow the verbosity level defined in the table mentioned earlier, but it is a relatively close correlation.

For detailed information about mute categories, refer to the `errlevel.h` file linked earlier. The mute level is the second number defined for each entry. The following screenshot shows some of the mute categories and verbosity levels:

```
● ● ●                                author@example
#define D_X509_ATTR          LOGLEV(4, 59, 0)        /* show x509-track attributes on connection */
#define D_INIT_MEDIUM        LOGLEV(4, 60, 0)        /* show medium frequency init messages */
#define D_MTU_INFO           LOGLEV(4, 61, 0)        /* show terse MTU info */
#define D_PID_DEBUG_LOW      LOGLEV(4, 63, 0)        /* show low-freq packet-id debugging info */
#define D_PID_DEBUG_MEDIUM   LOGLEV(4, 64, 0)        /* show medium-freq packet-id debugging info */

#define D_LOG_RW             LOGLEV(5, 0,  0)        /* Print 'R' or 'W' to stdout for read/write */

#define D_LINK_RW            LOGLEV(6, 69, M_DEBUG)  /* show TCP/UDP reads/writes (terse) */
#define D_TUN_RW             LOGLEV(6, 69, M_DEBUG)  /* show TUN/TAP reads/writes */
#define D_TAP_WIN_DEBUG      LOGLEV(6, 69, M_DEBUG)  /* show TAP-Windows driver debug info */
#define D_CLIENT_NAT         LOGLEV(6, 69, M_DEBUG)  /* show client NAT debug info */

#define D_SHOW_KEYS          LOGLEV(7, 70, M_DEBUG)  /* show data channel encryption keys */
#define D_SHOW_KEY_SOURCE    LOGLEV(7, 70, M_DEBUG)  /* show data channel key source entropy */
#define D_REL_LOW            LOGLEV(7, 70, M_DEBUG)  /* show low frequency info from reliable layer */
#define D_FRAG_DEBUG         LOGLEV(7, 70, M_DEBUG)  /* show fragment debugging info */
#define D_WIN32_IO_LOW       LOGLEV(7, 70, M_DEBUG)  /* low freq win32 I/O debugging info */
#define D_MTU_DEBUG          LOGLEV(7, 70, M_DEBUG)  /* show MTU debugging info */
#define D_MULTI_DEBUG        LOGLEV(7, 70, M_DEBUG)  /* show medium-freq multi debugging info */
#define D_MSS                LOGLEV(7, 70, M_DEBUG)  /* show MSS adjustments */
#define D_COMP_LOW           LOGLEV(7, 70, M_DEBUG)  /* show adaptive compression state changes */
#define D_CONNECTION_LIST    LOGLEV(7, 70, M_DEBUG)  /* show <connection> list info */
#define D_SCRIPT             LOGLEV(7, 70, M_DEBUG)  /* show parms & env vars passed to scripts */
#define D_SHOW_NET           LOGLEV(7, 70, M_DEBUG)  /* show routing table and adapter list */
#define D_ROUTE_DEBUG        LOGLEV(7, 70, M_DEBUG)  /* show verbose route.[ch] output */
#define D_TLS_STATE_ERRORS   LOGLEV(7, 70, M_DEBUG)  /* no TLS state for client */
#define D_SEMAPHORE_LOW      LOGLEV(7, 70, M_DEBUG)  /* show Win32 semaphore waits (low freq) */
#define D_SEMAPHORE          LOGLEV(7, 70, M_DEBUG)  /* show Win32 semaphore waits */
#define D_TEST_FILE          LOGLEV(7, 70, M_DEBUG)  /* show test_file() calls */
#define D_MANAGEMENT_DEBUG   LOGLEV(3, 70, M_DEBUG)  /* show --management debug info */
#define D_PLUGIN_DEBUG       LOGLEV(7, 70, M_DEBUG)  /* show verbose plugin calls */
#define D_SOCKET_DEBUG       LOGLEV(7, 70, M_DEBUG)  /* show socket.[ch] debugging info */
#define D_SHOW_PKCS11        LOGLEV(7, 70, M_DEBUG)  /* show PKCS#11 actions */
#define D_ALIGN_DEBUG        LOGLEV(7, 70, M_DEBUG)  /* show verbose struct alignment info */
#define D_PACKET_TRUNC_DEBUG LOGLEV(7, 70, M_DEBUG)  /* PACKET_TRUNCATION_CHECK verbose */
```

Contents of errlevel.h showing verbosity levels and mute category definitions

The `--mute` directive can be very useful on embedded devices where log storage is at a premium, or disk writes are considered *expensive* tasks. It is generally recommended to remove or omit it, however, when debugging a problematic VPN setup.

Apart from the normal event log, OpenVPN provides a separate log file used to indicate the current set of connected clients along with some connection details:

```
--status file [n]
```

This log is useful to help identify OpenVPN internal routes, connection time, remote and VPN IP addresses, and more.

The book *Mastering OpenVPN* includes some detailed examples of how to track connections and store them in a database in the seventh chapter named *Scripting and Plugins*.

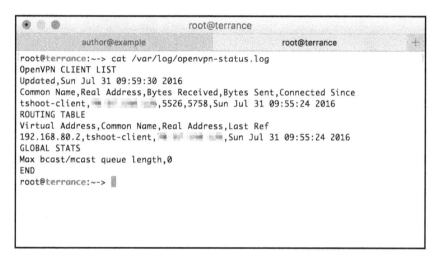

OpenVPN status log output

There are three distinct versions of the `--status-file`, the default being version one (shown earlier). Version two includes additional data fields while retaining the comma separation of the version one file. The version three file includes the same data as version two, but replaces the comma separator with a tab delimiter:

```
--status-version [n]
```

Logging levels

The ability to vary the verbosity of log output is useful when switching between a troubleshooting session and a normal operational session. The default logging level of 1 provides some useful informational logging level of 1 provides some useful informational logs along with the fatal errors indicative of a problem.

As of this writing, there are 108 different logging defines in the source, covered through 11 distinct verbosity levels. The majority of troubleshooting at an administrative level I've seen has not needed to go past verbosity 4 though there are exceptions, like when a firewall issue is suspected.

The following table provides a brief description of each level and provides the primary key log messages provided at that level. After the table, log samples showing a few different key levels are provided to illustrate the level of detail:

[n]	Included messages at verbosity level
0	Only fatal errors are logged.
1	Informational messages are also logged. Most critical task errors are `link`, `tls`, `resolver`, and `push`.
2	Additional informational messages: handshake, socket/interface close, and proxy errors.
3	Additional informational messages: `routes`, `auth`, `plugin`, `--port-share` messages, `ifconfig`, and filter data, management console debugging information.
4	Additional informational messages: runtime parameters, options compatibility, DHCP options, filter dropped packets, some **maximum transmission unit** (**MTU**) data. Verbosity level 4 is the most useful in the majority of troubleshooting scenarios.
5	R and W characters are written to the log for each packet that is sent and received. Lower case r and w characters are used for TUN/TAP packets.
6	Like verbosity 5, but `READ` and `WRITE` are used for TCP/UDP packets and lower case characters are used for TUN/TAP packets. Client NAT and TAP-Windows adapter debug information is included.
7	Crypto and tunnel debug information. Channel keys and entropy, compression debugging information, verbose routing information, much more.
8	Most process and schedule debugging, reliable routing debugging information.
9	Detailed tunnel and crypto data. Packet content prior to and post encryption is written, **PKCS#11**, TCP stream debug.

| 10 | Traffic shaping debug information. |
| 11 | Win32 registry debugging, OpenSSL lock information. |

The complete list of verbosity levels and the messages logged is available in the OpenVPN source code in `src/openvpn/errlevel.h`.

You can view the source on GitHub at `https://github.com/OpenVPN/openvpn/blob/master/src/openvpn/errlevel.h`.

For our examples here, we're using the following configurations. We have created a demonstration CA and certificates needed already:

Server:

```
dh dh1024.pem
dev tun
server 192.168.80.0 255.255.255.0
ca ca.crt
cert tshoot-server.crt
key tshoot-server.key
topology subnet
status /var/log/openvpn-status.log 5
keepalive 10 60
```

Client:

```
client
dev tun
proto udp
port 1194
remote 192.168.19.37

<ca>
-----BEGIN CERTIFICATE-----
CA PAYLOAD REMOVED
-----END CERTIFICATE-----
</ca>
<cert>
-----BEGIN CERTIFICATE-----
CERTIFICATE PAYLOAD REMOVED
-----END CERTIFICATE-----
</cert>
<key>
-----BEGIN PRIVATE KEY-----
KEY PAYLOAD REMOVED
-----END PRIVATE KEY-----
</key>
```

These same configurations, with noted option changes, will be used throughout this book. As above, certificate and key payload data will be omitted elsewhere for brevity.

For the screenshots given later, any changes to configuration of the client or server will be evident in the command-line options used and will be provided. Also, both screenshots will be taken after the server has started up and the client has connected. Deviations from this will be described, as in the case of attempting a connection to a known offline server for the purposes of demonstration.

Verbosity 0

Verbosity level 0 will only include messages deemed *fatal*. These will be errors that will prevent the VPN from functioning properly or may indicate severe security problems.

Server:

```
author@server:~-> openvpn --config openvpn.conf --verb 0
```

The preceding command gives the following output:

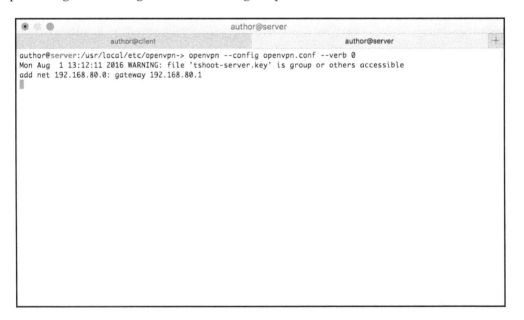

The preceding logs displayed show a warning for the permissions set on the private key for the X.509 certificate used by the OpenVPN server. The OpenVPN process wants Unix permissions of 500 or 600, and we have 644. Also logged is the defining of the route to our

VPN with the kernel (we used `192.168.80.0/24`).

Notably absent from the output is any indication that a client has connected. As evident later, however, we did connect a client.

Client:

```
author@client:~-> sudo openvpn/openvpn --config config.ovpn --verb 0
```

The preceding command gives the following output:

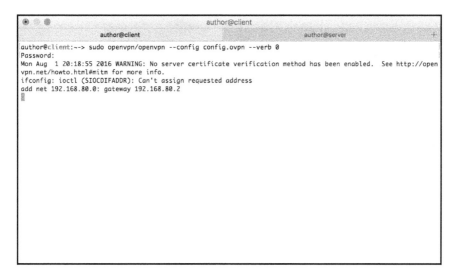

The client log is also rather sparse. We get a security-related warning about certificate verification method not being set (see `--ns-cert-type` and `--remote-cert-tls` for further details). We also see an error about a failed `ifconfig` command execution. Further details about what command was run and the results of the failure are not apparent at this level, we will need further details.

Finally, as with the server log, we see the setting of the route for the VPN within the kernel.

Verbosity 1

Increasing the verbosity from a 0 to the default of 1 reveals considerably more log entries in our sample connection. Information about OpenVPN version, compilation options, and SSL library version information is displayed.

 The screenshots and console output will show author@client or author@server. In most cases, this is a cosmetic affect for the sake of this book, and privileges are likely root and sudo are unnecessary.

Server:

```
author@server:~-> openvpn --config openvpn.conf --verb 1
```

The preceding command gives the following output:

```
                                    author@server
            author@client                    *              author@server              +
author@server:/usr/local/etc/openvpn-> openvpn --config openvpn.conf --verb 1
Mon Aug  1 14:28:33 2016 OpenVPN 2.3.11 amd64-portbld-freebsd10.1 [SSL (OpenSSL)] [LZO] [MH] [IPv6] built on J
ul 26 2016
Mon Aug  1 14:28:33 2016 library versions: OpenSSL 1.0.1j-freebsd 15 Oct 2014, LZO 2.09
Mon Aug  1 14:28:33 2016 WARNING: file 'tshoot-server.key' is group or others accessible
Mon Aug  1 14:28:33 2016 TUN/TAP device /dev/tun0 opened
Mon Aug  1 14:28:33 2016 do_ifconfig, tt->ipv6=0, tt->did_ifconfig_ipv6_setup=0
Mon Aug  1 14:28:33 2016 /sbin/ifconfig tun0 192.168.80.1 192.168.80.2 mtu 1500 netmask 255.255.255.0 up
add net 192.168.80.0: gateway 192.168.80.1
Mon Aug  1 14:28:33 2016 UDPv4 link local (bound): [undef]
Mon Aug  1 14:28:33 2016 UDPv4 link remote: [undef]
Mon Aug  1 14:28:33 2016 Initialization Sequence Completed
Mon Aug  1 14:28:45 2016 192.168.19.104:1194 [tshoot-client] Peer Connection Initiated with [AF_INET]192.168.1
9.104:1194
Mon Aug  1 14:28:45 2016 tshoot-client/192.168.19.104:1194 MULTI_sva: pool returned IPv4=192.168.80.2, IPv6=(N
ot enabled)
Mon Aug  1 14:28:47 2016 tshoot-client/192.168.19.104:1194 send_push_reply(): safe_cap=940
```

From the server logs, we can still see our security warning about permissions on the private key file. We also see more detailed information about the device used (`/dev/tun0`), the IP address assignment to the virtual interface, and a final startup message, `Initialization Sequence Completed`. This phrase in both the client and server logs indicates that the OpenVPN is up and running and is generally capable of passing traffic.

Once the server process was initialized, we connected the client. The server log show the evidence of the remote IP address from which the client connected and the **common name** (**CN**) of the client certificate.

The final line of the log is an informational message about the safe capacity for the `PUSH_REPLY` message from the client. This message may possibly come in handy when troubleshooting MTU problems:

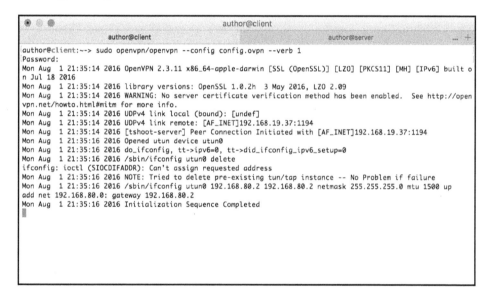

As with the server log, the previous error of the missing certificate verification method is listed at the increased verbosity. The IP and port of the remote server is listed along with the local virtual interface (`utun0`, the client is a Mac).

Like the certificate error, the failed `ifconfig` message is still present; only this time we see the reason. OpenVPN attempts to remove the old interface if it already exists. In our case, that interface is not present, so the `ifconfig` command naturally fails. The subsequent log message states this failure is not a problem.

Finally, the functional `ifconfig` command is parroted, the kernel routing entry add is displayed, and the `Initialization Sequence Completed` message is outputted. This line in both the server and client context means that the VPN tunnel has been created and is functional. Note that this does not mean all options and arguments were successfully implemented, just that there were no fatal errors. Routes may not be set, or there may be other setup issues.

Verbosity 4

Setting verbosity up to 4 greatly increases the volume of messages sent to the log. Upon execution, OpenVPN parses all of the configuration options and prints the list of options and functional arguments.

Server:

```
author@server:~-> openvpn --config openvpn.conf --verb 4
```

The preceding command gives the following output:

```
●  ●  ●                          author@server
Mon Aug  1 15:39:23 2016 us=373116 OpenVPN 2.3.11 amd64-portbld-freebsd10.1 [SSL (OpenSSL)] [LZO] [MH] [IPv6]
built on Jul 26 2016
Mon Aug  1 15:39:23 2016 us=373135 library versions: OpenSSL 1.0.1j-freebsd 15 Oct 2014, LZO 2.09
Mon Aug  1 15:39:23 2016 us=374191 Diffie-Hellman initialized with 1024 bit key
Mon Aug  1 15:39:23 2016 us=374412 WARNING: file 'tshoot-server.key' is group or others accessible
Mon Aug  1 15:39:23 2016 us=374649 TLS-Auth MTU parms [ L:1541 D:1212 EF:38 EB:0 ET:0 EL:3 ]
Mon Aug  1 15:39:23 2016 us=374668 Socket Buffers: R=[42080->42080] S=[9216->9216]
Mon Aug  1 15:39:23 2016 us=374894 TUN/TAP device /dev/tun0 opened
Mon Aug  1 15:39:23 2016 us=374904 do_ifconfig, tt->ipv6=0, tt->did_ifconfig_ipv6_setup=0
Mon Aug  1 15:39:23 2016 us=374920 /sbin/ifconfig tun0 192.168.80.1 192.168.80.2 mtu 1500 netmask 255.255.255.
0 up
Mon Aug  1 15:39:23 2016 us=377067 /sbin/route add -net 192.168.80.0 192.168.80.1 255.255.255.0
add net 192.168.80.0: gateway 192.168.80.1
Mon Aug  1 15:39:23 2016 us=380078 Data Channel MTU parms [ L:1541 D:1450 EF:41 EB:12 ET:0 EL:3 ]
Mon Aug  1 15:39:23 2016 us=381464 UDPv4 link local (bound): [undef]
Mon Aug  1 15:39:23 2016 us=381473 UDPv4 link remote: [undef]
Mon Aug  1 15:39:23 2016 us=381480 MULTI: multi_init called, r=256 v=256
Mon Aug  1 15:39:23 2016 us=381511 IFCONFIG POOL: base=192.168.80.2 size=252, ipv6=0
Mon Aug  1 15:39:23 2016 us=381530 Initialization Sequence Completed
Mon Aug  1 15:43:27 2016 us=392635 MULTI: multi_create_instance called
Mon Aug  1 15:43:27 2016 us=392689 192.168.19.104:1194 Re-using SSL/TLS context
Mon Aug  1 15:43:27 2016 us=392839 192.168.19.104:1194 Control Channel MTU parms [ L:1541 D:1212 EF:38 EB:0 ET
:0 EL:3 ]
Mon Aug  1 15:43:27 2016 us=392850 192.168.19.104:1194 Data Channel MTU parms [ L:1541 D:1450 EF:41 EB:12 ET:0
 EL:3 ]
Mon Aug  1 15:43:27 2016 us=392882 192.168.19.104:1194 Local Options String: 'V4,dev-type tun,link-mtu 1541,tu
n-mtu 1500,proto UDPv4,cipher BF-CBC,auth SHA1,keysize 128,key-method 2,tls-server'
Mon Aug  1 15:43:27 2016 us=392889 192.168.19.104:1194 Expected Remote Options String: 'V4,dev-type tun,link-m
tu 1541,tun-mtu 1500,proto UDPv4,cipher BF-CBC,auth SHA1,keysize 128,key-method 2,tls-client'
Mon Aug  1 15:43:27 2016 us=392909 192.168.19.104:1194 Local Options hash (VER=V4): '239669a8'
Mon Aug  1 15:43:27 2016 us=392919 192.168.19.104:1194 Expected Remote Options hash (VER=V4): '3514370b'
Mon Aug  1 15:43:27 2016 us=392949 192.168.19.104:1194 TLS: Initial packet from [AF_INET]192.168.19.104:1194,
sid=67dc26b2 49eefb82
Mon Aug  1 15:43:27 2016 us=403800 192.168.19.104:1194 VERIFY OK: depth=1, C=US, ST=Minnesota, L=St Paul, O=Tr
ouble Shooting OpenVPN, CN=Trouble Shooting OpenVPN, emailAddress=ecrist@secure-computing.net
Mon Aug  1 15:43:27 2016 us=403891 192.168.19.104:1194 VERIFY OK: depth=0, C=US, ST=Minnesota, O=Trouble Shoot
ing OpenVPN, CN=tshoot-client, emailAddress=ecrist@secure-computing.net
Mon Aug  1 15:43:27 2016 us=405790 192.168.19.104:1194 Data Channel Encrypt: Cipher 'BF-CBC' initialized with
128 bit key
Mon Aug  1 15:43:27 2016 us=405804 192.168.19.104:1194 Data Channel Encrypt: Using 160 bit message hash 'SHA1'
 for HMAC authentication
Mon Aug  1 15:43:27 2016 us=405843 192.168.19.104:1194 Data Channel Decrypt: Cipher 'BF-CBC' initialized with
128 bit key
Mon Aug  1 15:43:27 2016 us=405850 192.168.19.104:1194 Data Channel Decrypt: Using 160 bit message hash 'SHA1'
 for HMAC authentication
Mon Aug  1 15:43:27 2016 us=407115 192.168.19.104:1194 Control Channel: TLSv1.2, cipher TLSv1/SSLv3 DHE-RSA-AE
S256-GCM-SHA384, 1024 bit RSA
Mon Aug  1 15:43:27 2016 us=407135 192.168.19.104:1194 [tshoot-client] Peer Connection Initiated with [AF_INET
]192.168.19.104:1194
Mon Aug  1 15:43:27 2016 us=407155 tshoot-client/192.168.19.104:1194 MULTI_sva: pool returned IPv4=192.168.80.
2, IPv6=(Not enabled)
Mon Aug  1 15:43:27 2016 us=407183 tshoot-client/192.168.19.104:1194 MULTI: Learn: 192.168.80.2 -> tshoot-clie
nt/192.168.19.104:1194
Mon Aug  1 15:43:27 2016 us=407191 tshoot-client/192.168.19.104:1194 MULTI: primary virtual IP for tshoot-clie
nt/192.168.19.104:1194: 192.168.80.2
Mon Aug  1 15:43:29 2016 us=447391 tshoot-client/192.168.19.104:1194 PUSH: Received control message: 'PUSH_REQ
UEST'
Mon Aug  1 15:43:29 2016 us=447412 tshoot-client/192.168.19.104:1194 send_push_reply(): safe_cap=940
Mon Aug  1 15:43:29 2016 us=447429 tshoot-client/192.168.19.104:1194 SENT CONTROL [tshoot-client]: 'PUSH_REPLY
,route-gateway 192.168.80.1,topology subnet,ping 10,ping-restart 60,ifconfig 192.168.80.2 255.255.255.0' (stat
us=1)
```

With OpenVPN 2.3.11, the client startup produced 275 lines of options entries and the server startup produced 226 lines. Those lines are omitted from the following screenshots to discuss the more useful lines that follow.

The startup of the OpenVPN server process looks very similar at verbosity 4 as it does at level 1, apart from the appearance of the runtime options and configuration. Once the client actually connects, however, there is a significant amount of details provided.

Upon client connection, remote and local options are compared and messages are displayed about compatibility. If there are differences, such as tun versus tap, the errors will show up here. Also listed, are encryption cipher details. We can see that BF-CBC (see https://en.wikipedia.org/wiki/Blowfish_(cipher) for further details) with a 160 bit SHA1 message hash for HMAC authentication for the data channel. Finally, the control channel is using TLSv1.2 with DHE-RSA-AES256-GCM-SHA384 with a 1024 bit RSA key.

Upon termination of the OpenVPN process, messages about closing the device, socket, and destruction of the interface are indicated. Also, the reason for the exit is shown, in our case a SIGINT, caused by my *Ctrl* + *C* on the console.

Client:

```
author@client:~-> sudo openvpn/openvpn --config config.ovpn --verb 4
```

The client logs also show quite a bit of certificate detail at verbosity level 4. Within the log, we can see the same data channel encryption setup using BF-CBC with 128-bit keys, HMAC message hash using 160-bit SHA1. As indicated on the server, the control channel is using TLSv1.2 with DHE-RSA-AES256-GCM-SHA384 and a 1024-bit RSA key.

Further through the negotiation, we can see the details of `PUSH REQUEST/PUSH REPLY` and the interface and routing setup. We also still see the `ifconfig` command failure (which still isn't a problem):

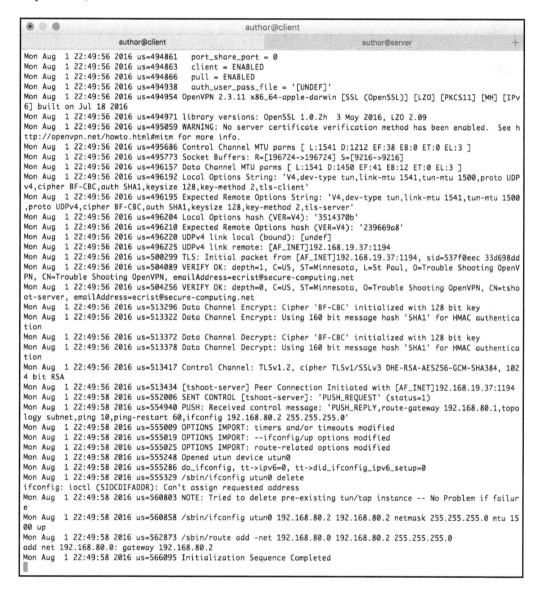

One indicator of a firewall problem is the `RWRW` pattern, or lack of, in the log file. For example, a working ping transaction between two systems will show both `R` and `W` in the log file. When the remote endpoint is blocking the traffic, you will only see `W` in the log file and can identify a notable lack of the `R` entries.

Verbosity 7

When we increase the verbosity once more from `4` up to `7`, we get much of the same details on startup we're accustom to at `4` and below. In addition, we will see some notably dense information surrounding cryptographic activities, including encryption and decryption keys used (server log only).

Server:

```
author@server:~-> openvpn --config openvpn.conf --verb 7
```

The detail at `--verb 7` is too great to show in full via a screenshot, so the part of the information deemed most useful is shown here. The full log for both the client and server will be available on the Packt website.

As you can see in the illustration later, there is quite a bit of private information that should be protected. The keys displayed can be used to later decrypt the traffic that used those keys.

It should not be necessary to use this level of debugging information unless you are testing new and/or as-yet unsupported cryptographic ciphers or actually working on OpenVPN development. The typical system administrator will likely not have much use for the amount of data available:

```
●  ●  ●                          author@server

Tue Aug   2 15:12:35 2016 us=438387 192.168.19.104:1194 Client random2: ad16a164 bb53619e 4d697e01 212ec316 c36
6a4b7 9e227764 071402f5 8ff02af7
Tue Aug   2 15:12:35 2016 us=438399 192.168.19.104:1194 Server pre_master: 00000000 00000000 00000000 00000000
00000000 00000000 00000000 00000000 00000000 00000000 00000000 00000000
Tue Aug   2 15:12:35 2016 us=438406 192.168.19.104:1194 Server random1: 822d6714 0de9538a aa7ffa60 6e70e493 106
05ec0 e96c26a4 94f2e083 44fae145
Tue Aug   2 15:12:35 2016 us=438414 192.168.19.104:1194 Server random2: 027b3fce a4f431bd 5dcd3472 02928993 14d
f8f61 2b23e947 6cefbe1f d6ac355e
Tue Aug   2 15:12:35 2016 us=438423 192.168.19.104:1194 tls1_P_hash sec: f2406a15 efdb3c61 0ba911a8 d8b7adf6 9e
534096 0a10fa88
Tue Aug   2 15:12:35 2016 us=438440 192.168.19.104:1194 tls1_P_hash seed: 4f70656e 56504e20 6d617374 65722073 6
5637265 74d70eec ae0c30e5 15770fea 706f3747 a5145c71 414801b2 31fbf831 2ba9fa12 6e822d67 140de953 8aaa7ffa 606
e70e4 9310605e c0e96c26 a494f2e0 8344fae1 45
Tue Aug   2 15:12:35 2016 us=438460 192.168.19.104:1194 tls1_P_hash out: f56e5fdb e400dc82 45599733 58925f78 94
b25596 fdd3333d 1b2ca168 db52a596 03a02103 4bd36d1c 2369aa1a a0618072
Tue Aug   2 15:12:35 2016 us=438467 192.168.19.104:1194 tls1_P_hash sec: fc113ff6 dad73412 c05d48cc 1a038028 0a
e948ce 269b7502
Tue Aug   2 15:12:35 2016 us=438483 192.168.19.104:1194 tls1_P_hash seed: 4f70656e 56504e20 6d617374 65722073 6
5637265 74d70eec ae0c30e5 15770fea 706f3747 a5145c71 414801b2 31fbf831 2ba9fa12 6e822d67 140de953 8aaa7ffa 606
e70e4 9310605e c0e96c26 a494f2e0 8344fae1 45
Tue Aug   2 15:12:35 2016 us=438531 192.168.19.104:1194 tls1_P_hash out: 6779011e 00af0cbf 846c8ef8 831eb4a4 91
27e592 c4ac6a24 c4529d56 77fb1d55 8664084b c2120bd7 c357e09c f2f16e60
Tue Aug   2 15:12:35 2016 us=438543 192.168.19.104:1194 tls1_PRF out[48]: 92175ec5 e4afd03d c13519cb db8cebdc 0
595b004 397f5919 df7e3c3e aca9b8c3 85c42948 89c166cb e03e4a86 5290ee12
Tue Aug   2 15:12:35 2016 us=438551 192.168.19.104:1194 tls1_P_hash sec: 92175ec5 e4afd03d c13519cb db8cebdc 05
95b004 397f5919
Tue Aug   2 15:12:35 2016 us=438570 192.168.19.104:1194 tls1_P_hash seed: 4f70656e 56504e20 6b657920 65787061 6
e73696f 6ead16a1 64bb5361 9e4d697e 01212ec3 16c366a4 b79e2277 64071402 f58ff02a f7027b3f cea4f431 bd5dcd34 720
29289 9314df8f 612b23e9 476cefbe 1fd6ac35 5e3f06bd 58c38824 62a2918d f057d15c e9
Tue Aug   2 15:12:35 2016 us=438630 192.168.19.104:1194 tls1_P_hash out: b1242735 56aa5925 7c7e257b daadb0c1 b5
e5c99c 5374d633 1d8adfd3 ac85e970 e344b187 1ef413e2 adf07701 88be7090 6ac2e624 daf2a452 645a867b 1b4d0949 0661
623c 721f27b7 504526c6 f824d8aa c42d7d02 091fe984 3630f6dd ea87c973 5abed900 b3450835 40854a59 6a6c6ea7 578e5f
fa 1f0420fb c230543d e6f82bde b970bd69 d5762469 3b72cc65 bbe86f9a fe426399 d5575bd8 3cc4e061 a7eddd07 c9f9e31a
9a42c667 2f4a3473 43e414d1 1b7a7fdb 0e1b5c96 aaeb582f 93cfb524 d44366a4 a05d47f8 0142016c 6ac4ad33 df2b310a 6
b03acf6 bb4f30e0 edbe4b3a 8c4fe05d 419d3fe6 f323ae70 8de186c7 2a481620 5b9a2ea9 106cb03c b2dd1a67
Tue Aug   2 15:12:35 2016 us=438637 192.168.19.104:1194 tls1_P_hash sec: df7e3c3e aca9b8c3 85c42948 89c166cb e0
3e4a86 5290ee12
Tue Aug   2 15:12:35 2016 us=438656 192.168.19.104:1194 tls1_P_hash seed: 4f70656e 56504e20 6b657920 65787061 6
e73696f 6ead16a1 64bb5361 9e4d697e 01212ec3 16c366a4 b79e2277 64071402 f58ff02a f7027b3f cea4f431 bd5dcd34 720
29289 9314df8f 612b23e9 476cefbe 1fd6ac35 5e3f06bd 58c38824 62a2918d f057d15c e9
Tue Aug   2 15:12:35 2016 us=438735 192.168.19.104:1194 tls1_P_hash out: 54b9d541 29676a95 dbda6e1e 3e5c7853 41
191c1a 8548de0f 82cc0f33 8c5e8e36 a66e0037 77998889 7984a580 7c2a3cd5 c705e9ce 4f7121b0 2b97d288 a82f7055 b7ea
88dc 4e9c7e6e 1ac6b87c 6b6eaf9a 0d2a2ca8 bc9ec5de 326c85dc 7a8898f3 9e39b0e0 d5c15429 14c611b2 24957676 fa6f47
0c e40ab882 7dc59312 3c3e1548 93d82018 1821f00f 5be6331e 49096a81 4be3f0fe 06a32509 88218c85 35147820 d277e8aa
1e805cdd 929dd3af 15b7e675 04d4f249 c2c77cb1 c7909da7 4cbc9126 c4c5a858 a966fda1 d51f5180 c53ab0db cf65a8b7 c
c14f886 a82d1fc7 de5e80c9 2d166086 0bab684f cbf2f398 80214c15 b7e7231f 0f6906d4 b40bac03 72b28ae4
Tue Aug   2 15:12:35 2016 us=438779 192.168.19.104:1194 tls1_PRF out[256]: e59df274 7fcd33b0 a7a44b65 e4f1c892
f4fcd586 d63c083c 9f46d0e0 20db6746 452ab1b0 696d9b6b d474d281 f4944c45 adc70fea 958385e2 4fcd54f3 b362791c b1
8beae0 3c8359d9 4a839eba 934a7730 c90751aa b5812c5a 045c7301 900f5180 c48769e0 66845c1c 54435beb 4ef918d1 ade1
18f6 fb0e9879 bff5c72f dac63e96 2aa89d71 cd57d466 6094ff7b f2e1051b b5a19367 d3f47ed1 b4e56ce4 92f9a527 1b8e0b
b0 84c29aba bdd7e7dc 5653f2a4 1fae8d92 ccdc2027 6d7bc588 df732402 1086cefc 093bba59 d45d50ec affe1de8 104e99bd
a7175470 13622f27 33e0cbf3 a15980db 4a3657a9 38d15de8 0dc0cad2 9daf353f 54f3287d a4671c3f c06f9083
Tue Aug   2 15:12:35 2016 us=438785 192.168.19.104:1194 Master Encrypt (cipher): e59df274 7fcd33b0 a7a44b65 e4f
1c892
Tue Aug   2 15:12:35 2016 us=438791 192.168.19.104:1194 Master Encrypt (hmac): b18beae0 3c8359d9 4a839eba 934a7
730 c90751aa
Tue Aug   2 15:12:35 2016 us=438797 192.168.19.104:1194 Master Decrypt (cipher): 2aa89d71 cd57d466 6094ff7b f2e
1051b
Tue Aug   2 15:12:35 2016 us=438803 192.168.19.104:1194 Master Decrypt (hmac): 1086cefc 093bba59 d45d50ec affe1
de8 104e99bd
Tue Aug   2 15:12:35 2016 us=438806 192.168.19.104:1194 CRYPTO INFO: n_DES_cblocks=0
Tue Aug   2 15:12:35 2016 us=438810 192.168.19.104:1194 CRYPTO INFO: n_DES_cblocks=0
```

A subset of logging output at –verb 7 showing actual cryptographic keys and seed data

Client:

```
author@client:~-> sudo openvpn/openvpn --config config.ovpn --verb 7
```

The preceding command gives the following output:

```
author@client
Tue Aug  2 22:19:05 2016 us=376674 UDPv4 READ [247] from [AF_INET]192.168.19.37:1194: P_CONTROL_V1 kid=0 [ 4 ]
 pid=5 DATA len=221
Tue Aug  2 22:19:05 2016 us=376835 Data Channel Encrypt: Cipher 'BF-CBC' initialized with 128 bit key
Tue Aug  2 22:19:05 2016 us=376844 Data Channel Encrypt: Using 160 bit message hash 'SHA1' for HMAC authentica
tion
Tue Aug  2 22:19:05 2016 us=376891 Data Channel Decrypt: Cipher 'BF-CBC' initialized with 128 bit key
Tue Aug  2 22:19:05 2016 us=376900 Data Channel Decrypt: Using 160 bit message hash 'SHA1' for HMAC authentica
tion
Tue Aug  2 22:19:05 2016 us=376918 UDPv4 WRITE [22] to [AF_INET]192.168.19.37:1194: P_ACK_V1 kid=0 [ 5 ]
Tue Aug  2 22:19:05 2016 us=376949 Control Channel: TLSv1.2, cipher TLSv1/SSLv3 DHE-RSA-AES256-GCM-SHA384, 102
4 bit RSA
Tue Aug  2 22:19:05 2016 us=376965 [tshoot-server] Peer Connection Initiated with [AF_INET]192.168.19.37:1194
Tue Aug  2 22:19:07 2016 us=539700 SENT CONTROL [tshoot-server]: 'PUSH_REQUEST' (status=1)
Tue Aug  2 22:19:07 2016 us=539859 UDPv4 WRITE [56] to [AF_INET]192.168.19.37:1194: P_CONTROL_V1 kid=0 [ ] pid
=5 DATA len=42
Tue Aug  2 22:19:07 2016 us=542340 UDPv4 READ [22] from [AF_INET]192.168.19.37:1194: P_ACK_V1 kid=0 [ 5 ]
Tue Aug  2 22:19:07 2016 us=542405 UDPv4 READ [157] from [AF_INET]192.168.19.37:1194: P_CONTROL_V1 kid=0 [ ] p
id=6 DATA len=143
Tue Aug  2 22:19:07 2016 us=542441 PUSH: Received control message: 'PUSH_REPLY,route-gateway 192.168.80.1,topo
logy subnet,ping 10,ping-restart 60,ifconfig 192.168.80.2 255.255.255.0'
Tue Aug  2 22:19:07 2016 us=542489 OPTIONS IMPORT: timers and/or timeouts modified
Tue Aug  2 22:19:07 2016 us=542496 OPTIONS IMPORT: --ifconfig/up options modified
Tue Aug  2 22:19:07 2016 us=542502 OPTIONS IMPORT: route-related options modified
Tue Aug  2 22:19:07 2016 us=542705 Opened utun device utun0
Tue Aug  2 22:19:07 2016 us=542735 do_ifconfig, tt->ipv6=0, tt->did_ifconfig_ipv6_setup=0
Tue Aug  2 22:19:07 2016 us=542780 /sbin/ifconfig utun0 delete
ifconfig: ioctl (SIOCDIFADDR): Can't assign requested address
Tue Aug  2 22:19:07 2016 us=546044 NOTE: Tried to delete pre-existing tun/tap instance -- No Problem if failur
e
Tue Aug  2 22:19:07 2016 us=546098 /sbin/ifconfig utun0 192.168.80.2 192.168.80.2 netmask 255.255.255.0 mtu 15
00 up
Tue Aug  2 22:19:07 2016 us=548422 /sbin/route add -net 192.168.80.0 192.168.80.2 255.255.255.0
add net 192.168.80.0: gateway 192.168.80.2
Tue Aug  2 22:19:07 2016 us=551594 Initialization Sequence Completed
Tue Aug  2 22:19:07 2016 us=551639 UDPv4 WRITE [22] to [AF_INET]192.168.19.37:1194: P_ACK_V1 kid=0 [ 6 ]
Tue Aug  2 22:19:07 2016 us=809563 UDPv4 WRITE [125] to [AF_INET]192.168.19.37:1194: P_DATA_V1 kid=0 DATA len=
124
Tue Aug  2 22:19:07 2016 us=812080 UDPv4 READ [125] from [AF_INET]192.168.19.37:1194: P_DATA_V1 kid=0 DATA len
=124
Tue Aug  2 22:19:08 2016 us=814797 UDPv4 WRITE [125] to [AF_INET]192.168.19.37:1194: P_DATA_V1 kid=0 DATA len=
124
Tue Aug  2 22:19:08 2016 us=816178 UDPv4 READ [125] from [AF_INET]192.168.19.37:1194: P_DATA_V1 kid=0 DATA len
=124
^CTue Aug  2 22:19:11 2016 us=127329 event_wait : Interrupted system call (code=4)
Tue Aug  2 22:19:11 2016 us=127722 TCP/UDP: Closing socket
Tue Aug  2 22:19:11 2016 us=127878 Closing TUN/TAP interface
Tue Aug  2 22:19:11 2016 us=129653 SIGINT[hard,] received, process exiting
Tue Aug  2 22:19:11 2016 us=134388 PKCS#11: Terminating openssl
Tue Aug  2 22:19:11 2016 us=134412 PKCS#11: Removing providers
Tue Aug  2 22:19:11 2016 us=134419 PKCS#11: Releasing sessions
Tue Aug  2 22:19:11 2016 us=134424 PKCS#11: Marking as uninitialized
author@client:~->
```

When I ran the client, I noted that an error was displayed right away. The client I'm using to write this is the Tunnelblick (`https://tunnelblick.net`) build, which lacks debug support. The message was:

Tue Aug 2 22:19:05 2016 NOTE: debug verbosity (--verb 7) is enabled but this build lacks debug support.

Looking into the OpenVPN source, the `options.c` file (`https://git.io/v6kse`) on line 4885 indicates that either `ENABLE_SMALL` or `ENABLE_DEBUG` need to be enabled at compile time:

```
#if !defined(ENABLE_DEBUG) && !defined(ENABLE_SMALL)
      /* Warn when a debug verbosity is supplied when built
      without debug support */
   if (options->verbosity >= 7)
     msg (M_WARN, "NOTE: debug verbosity (--verb %d) is enabled
     but this build lacks debug support.",
        options->verbosity);
#endif
```

Examining the output of `./configure --help`, the first step to building OpenVPN, it is revealed that debug is enabled by default, but the Tunnelblick-supplied build was compiled with `--disable-debug`:

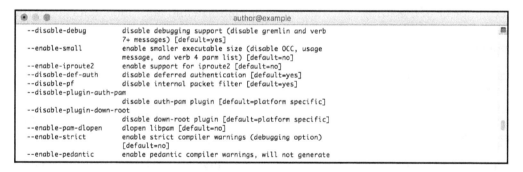

./configure –help output showing –disable-debug

The full output is considerably longer than what is shown. There are roughly 36 compile options, in addition to setting numerous options in order to set environment variables.

Strange problems can arise if the client and server are using significantly different compile-time options.

Common log messages

Understanding the most common log messages present at `--verb 4` allows you to quickly scan the log file for errors while also comprehending the events taking place. The messages described here are a mix of both affirmative (good) messages, as well as the most common messages indicating errors.

Startup messages

OpenVPN will evoke a number of messages upon startup. Some of these messages are informational, others are warnings of perhaps new options, or options that are potentially dangerous if used or omitted.

Version and compile string

The first line to explore is the OpenVPN version string. This string will indicate the actual release of the software used along with some important build and compile-time information. The first two examples show OpenVPN version 2.3.11 compiled with OpenSSL, LZO, PKCS11, MH (extended IP packet information), and IPv6.

The second piece of the string lists the processor platform and additional data about the system that performed the compile. Our first example shows a 64-bit system (`x86_64`), on an Apple system, with `darwin` as the indicated kernel version:

```
OpenVPN 2.3.11 x86_64-apple-darwin [SSL (OpenSSL)] [LZO] [PKCS11] [MH]
[IPv6] built on Jul 18 2016
```

The second example is also 64-bit (`amd64`, see note, later), built with the FreeBSD ports system (packager), with kernel from `freebsd10.1`:

OpenVPN 2.3.11 amd64-portbld-freebsd10.1 [SSL (OpenSSL)] [LZO] [MH] [IPv6] built on Jul 26 2016

If we look back to our compiled Raspberry Pi build on page six of `Chapter 3`, *Installing OpenVPN*, we can see a slightly different list of options. In this case, `PolarSSL` was used for the SSL library and `EPOLL` was enabled. What is missing from earlier is the `LZO` and `PKCS11` support. This system was compiled on a generic Linux system on `arm6l` (low-power ARM). Note that these differences don't yet indicate a real problem. These can help us identify where to start looking or which messages to seek out further into the logs:

OpenVPN 2.3.11 arm6l-unknown-linux-gnueabihf [SSL (PolarSSL)] [EPOLL] [MH] [IPv6] built on Jun 29 2016

The 64-bit architecture is referred to by many different monikers, determined generally by the time frame or initial system upon which development was started. All of the following are equivalent in meaning: x86-64, x86_64, x64, and amd64. The Itanium 64 architecture (ia_64), is a different architecture. Read more on Wikipedia at https://en.wikipedia.org/wiki/X86-64.

Option warnings

There are a few specific options OpenVPN looks for when starting up. For the clients, the first option defines the server certificate verification method. This is accomplished with the --remote-cert-tls [server|client] option. Without this option, OpenVPN will be unable to protect against a valid client certificate being used as a server certificate. Since they are all children of the same CA, it would be possible to use one client certificate to create a server instance posing as the official server, creating a **man-in-the-middle (MITM)** vulnerability:

> **WARNING: No server certificate verification method has been enabled. See http://openvpn.net/howto.html#mitm for more information.**

Another set of option warnings is presented when --script-security is set to level 2 or 3. At level 2, user-defined scripts can be called from within the configuration or command-line arguments:

> **NOTE: the current --script-security setting may allow this configuration to call user-defined scripts**

At level 3, user credentials, including passwords, are made available in the environment to the scripts defined:

> **WARNING: the current --script-security setting may allow passwords to be passed to scripts via environmental variables**

Finally, if a script is defined (in --up, --down, or others), and --script-security has not been set to allow user-defined scripts, the following message will be logged:

> **NOTE: starting with OpenVPN 2.1, '--script-security 2' or higher is required to call user-defined scripts or executables**

OpenVPN will alert you if there is an unrecognized option present within the configuration file or on the command line. Note that the application will exit immediately upon the first instance of an invalid configuration option.

In the following screenshot, we have added an invalid parameter, `fake-option`, to the `openvpn.conf` configuration file. In the first execution attempt, the application recognizes the option and outputs the file and line number: `openvpn.conf:10`, which is line 10 of the `openvpn.conf` file:

```
author@server:/usr/local/etc/openvpn-> openvpn --config openvpn.conf --verb 4
Options error: Unrecognized option or missing parameter(s) in openvpn.conf:10: fake-option (2.3.11)
Use --help for more information.
author@server:/usr/local/etc/openvpn-> openvpn --fake2 --config openvpn.conf --verb 4
Options error: Unrecognized option or missing parameter(s) in [CMD-LINE]:1: fake2 (2.3.11)
Use --help for more information.
author@server:/usr/local/etc/openvpn->
```

Showing output when invalid options are applied

The second execution applies the option `fake2` on the command line, before the configuration file is indicated. Instead of a file name, `[CMD-LINE]` is stated. The number `1` can be ignored as everything will be on line 1 for the command-line arguments.

Configuration parameters

There are a few messages displayed during initialization of the software that can later aid in troubleshooting. Some of these messages illustrate the effect settings used, as in the case of MTU data. Other messages are indicative of connection and setup progress.

There are two MTU-specific startup messages: one for the control channel and another for the data channel. The latter is the most common source of headache, as it's the channel used to transmit and encapsulate the actual traffic the VPN is used for:

Control Channel MTU parms [L:1541 D:1212 EF:38 EB:0 ET:0 EL:3]

The control channel is used to communicate between the OpenVPN instances at the local and remote ends. Configuration parameters such as `push` and `key negotiation`, all take place over this channel:

Data Channel MTU parms [L:1541 D:1450 EF:41 EB:12 ET:0 EL:3]

The fields present are useful to identify where the breakdown of communication occurs later. The fields are described in the table here. If you want full details about the data within the log message, and what it really means, you can find it at `http://build.openvpn.net/d` `oxygen/html/structframe.html`:

Field name	Description
Link MTU (L) `link_mtu`	Maximum packet size to be sent over the external interface. This is the physical interface (outside of OpenVPN's `tun` or `tap` device).
Link MTU Dynamic (D) `link_mtu_dynamic`	The dynamic MTU value for the external network interface. This is generally the usable packet size.
Extra Frame (EF) `extra_frame`	The maximum number of bytes that all processing can add to the frame header.
Extra Buffer (EB) `extra_buffer`	The maximum number of bytes processing may add to the internal work buffer.
Extra Tun Bytes (ET) `extra_tun`	The maximum number of bytes in excess of the TUN/TAP device MTU that may be read or written.
Extra Link Bytes (EL) `extra_link`	The maximum number of bytes in excess of the external interface MTU that may be read or written.

Arguably the most useful data points in the data is the Link MTU (L) and Dynamic MTU (D). More details on troubleshooting MTU path issues, see `Chapter 7`, *Network and Routing*.

LZO compression must be either enabled or disabled at both ends of the OpenVPN connection. If the following line is present on the server or the client, and missing from the other, the connection will ultimately fail:

LZO compression initialized

During a connection initialization, the both endpoints perform a remote options hash to determine compatibility of the other side in the context of configuration. When looking at the logs, the hash should match between both side.

Immediately, prior to the options has comparison, the expected remote and local configuration parameters are briefly listed. The parameters here can be used to quickly identify configuration mismatches between the two sides of the tunnel.

Server:

```
Local Options String: 'V4,dev-type tun,link-mtu 1541,tun-mtu 1500,proto
UDPv4,cipher BF-CBC,auth SHA1,keysize 128,key-method 2,tls-server'Expected
Remote Options String: 'V4,dev-type tun,link-mtu 1541,tun-mtu 1500,proto
UDPv4,cipher BF-CBC,auth SHA1,keysize 128,key-method 2,tls-client'Local
Options hash (VER=V4): '239669a8'Expected Remote Options hash (VER=V4):
'3514370b'
```

Client:

```
Local Options String: 'V4,dev-type tun,link-mtu 1541,tun-mtu 1500,proto
UDPv4,cipher BF-CBC,auth SHA1,keysize 128,key-method 2,tls-client'Expected
Remote Options String: 'V4,dev-type tun,link-mtu 1541,tun-mtu 1500,proto
UDPv4,cipher BF-CBC,auth SHA1,keysize 128,key-method 2,tls-server'Local
Options hash (VER=V4): '3514370b'Expected Remote Options hash (VER=V4):
'239669a8'
```

The final important message is the essential *all clear* from the startup routine. This message does not guarantee that you have a working and useful VPN, OpenVPN doesn't truly understand your entire routing table and the entirety of devices involved. This message simply illustrates that the OpenVPN process at both ends has successfully negotiated cryptographic keys, option parsing, and is prepared and ready to start doing the things you've asked of it:

Initialization Sequence Completed

Operational messages

During the use of the VPN, there will be a number of messages displayed, particularly at the higher verbosity levels. Routing errors, certificate verification, and other errors become apparent here.

Certificate messages

Particularly on the server, certificate messages will be displayed throughout the course of a running tunnel. Verification, **Certificate Revocation List** (**CRL**), and validity are performed upon each handshake. Both the server and client support the use of CRLs, but they are typically only used on the server side.

In the following screenshot, the highlighted text demonstrates a CRL check with a valid client certificate:

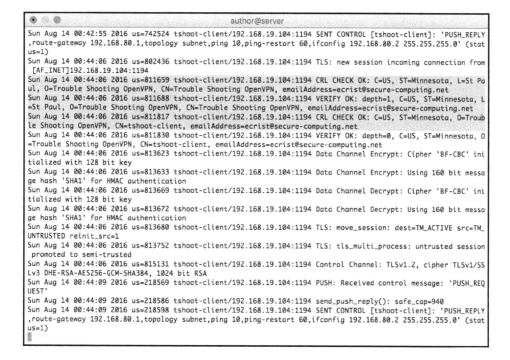

I've also created a separate certificate and revoked it, providing the updated `crl.pem` file to the OpenVPN process. When the client attempts to connect with the revoked certificate, we can see the **certificate authority (CA)** if validated (the first `CRL CHECK OK`) followed by the `CRL CHECK FAILED` for the `tshoot-revoke` certificate:

```
                               author@server
Sun Aug 14 00:49:18 2016 us=283108 Data Channel MTU parms [ L:1541 D:1450 EF:41 EB:12 ET:0 EL:3 ]
Sun Aug 14 00:49:18 2016 us=283155 UDPv4 link local (bound): [undef]
Sun Aug 14 00:49:18 2016 us=283162 UDPv4 link remote: [undef]
Sun Aug 14 00:49:18 2016 us=283169 MULTI: multi_init called, r=256 v=256
Sun Aug 14 00:49:18 2016 us=283193 IFCONFIG POOL: base=192.168.80.2 size=252, ipv6=0
Sun Aug 14 00:49:18 2016 us=283208 Initialization Sequence Completed
Sun Aug 14 00:53:53 2016 us=201262 MULTI: multi_create_instance called
Sun Aug 14 00:53:53 2016 us=201330 192.168.19.104:1194 Re-using SSL/TLS context
Sun Aug 14 00:53:53 2016 us=201463 192.168.19.104:1194 Control Channel MTU parms [ L:1541 D:1212 EF:38 EB:0 ET
:0 EL:3 ]
Sun Aug 14 00:53:53 2016 us=201473 192.168.19.104:1194 Data Channel MTU parms [ L:1541 D:1450 EF:41 EB:12 ET:0
 EL:3 ]
Sun Aug 14 00:53:53 2016 us=201511 192.168.19.104:1194 Local Options String: 'V4,dev-type tun,link-mtu 1541,tu
n-mtu 1500,proto UDPv4,cipher BF-CBC,auth SHA1,keysize 128,key-method 2,tls-server'
Sun Aug 14 00:53:53 2016 us=201518 192.168.19.104:1194 Expected Remote Options String: 'V4,dev-type tun,link-m
tu 1541,tun-mtu 1500,proto UDPv4,cipher BF-CBC,auth SHA1,keysize 128,key-method 2,tls-client'
Sun Aug 14 00:53:53 2016 us=201536 192.168.19.104:1194 Local Options hash (VER=V4): '239669a8'
Sun Aug 14 00:53:53 2016 us=201545 192.168.19.104:1194 Expected Remote Options hash (VER=V4): '3514370b'
Sun Aug 14 00:53:53 2016 us=201577 192.168.19.104:1194 TLS: Initial packet from [AF_INET]192.168.19.104:1194,
sid=09d92907 ad90e97d
Sun Aug 14 00:53:53 2016 us=212172 192.168.19.104:1194 CRL CHECK OK: C=US, ST=Minnesota, L=St Paul, O=Trouble
Shooting OpenVPN, CN=Trouble Shooting OpenVPN, emailAddress=ecrist@secure-computing.net
Sun Aug 14 00:53:53 2016 us=212198 192.168.19.104:1194 VERIFY OK: depth=1, C=US, ST=Minnesota, L=St Paul, O=Tr
ouble Shooting OpenVPN, CN=Trouble Shooting OpenVPN, emailAddress=ecrist@secure-computing.net
Sun Aug 14 00:53:53 2016 us=212319 192.168.19.104:1194 CRL CHECK FAILED: C=US, ST=Minnesota, O=Trouble Shootin
g OpenVPN, CN=tshoot-revoke, emailAddress=ecrist@secure-computing.net (serial 03) is REVOKED
Sun Aug 14 00:53:53 2016 us=212379 192.168.19.104:1194 OpenSSL: error:140890B2:SSL routines:SSL3_GET_CLIENT_CE
RTIFICATE:no certificate returned
Sun Aug 14 00:53:53 2016 us=212387 192.168.19.104:1194 TLS_ERROR: BIO read tls_read_plaintext error
Sun Aug 14 00:53:53 2016 us=212394 192.168.19.104:1194 TLS Error: TLS object -> incoming plaintext read error
Sun Aug 14 00:53:53 2016 us=212398 192.168.19.104:1194 TLS Error: TLS handshake failed
Sun Aug 14 00:53:53 2016 us=212469 192.168.19.104:1194 SIGUSR1[soft,tls-error] received, client-instance resta
rting
```

Unlike the OpenVPN configuration file, the CRL file is reread on every client connection and each time the TLS keys are renegotiated. The OpenVPN process is not aware, however, of when the file is updated, so clients that are revoked will need to be either killed via the management console, or they will be disconnected at the next re-key.

Apart from CRL-related messages, both the OpenVPN server and client will verify the certificate chain to ensure the remote side is using a valid certificate. In our test scenario, the certificate chain is pretty basic with a CA, and all signed certificates directly below it:

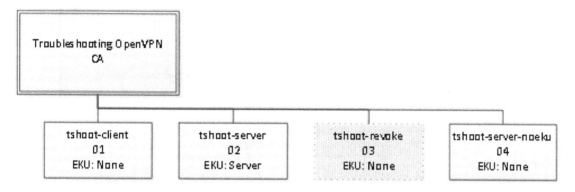

A sample certificate chain used for Troubleshooting OpenVPN

The first VERIFY log line indicates the depth as 1. This depth is from the view of the presented certificate by the server because this is the client log. The verification will proceed from the deepest certificate first, which is the signing authority.

Both sides have access to the CA certificate (via the --ca parameter), so can validate the signature. In this case, the validity is confirmed:

> **VERIFY OK: depth=1, C=US, ST=Minnesota, L=St Paul, O=Trouble Shooting OpenVPN, CN=Trouble Shooting OpenVPN, emailAddress=ecrist@secure-computing.net**

This process repeats all the way through the certificate chain to the server certificate (or the client certificate, in the case of the server performing the validation):

> **VERIFY OK: depth=0, C=US, ST=Minnesota, O=Trouble Shooting OpenVPN, CN=tshoot-server, emailAddress=ecrist@secure-computing.net**

You can see which certificate is being validated by looking at the CN= portion of the string. In our sample chain, I used Trouble Shooting OpenVPN for the certificate authority and tshoot-server for the server certificate.

When `--tls-remote-cert` is applied, additional log messages are printed, showing the verification of certificate usage. The first screenshot (note highlighted messages) displays a successful connection to a server with the extended key usage for server applied:

```
                          author@client
PN, CN=Trouble Shooting OpenVPN, emailAddress=ecrist@secure-computing.net
Sun Aug 14 08:33:32 2016 us=539781 Validating certificate key usage
Sun Aug 14 08:33:32 2016 us=539788 ++ Certificate has key usage  00a0, expects 00a0
Sun Aug 14 08:33:32 2016 us=539792 VERIFY KU OK
Sun Aug 14 08:33:32 2016 us=539797 Validating certificate extended key usage
Sun Aug 14 08:33:32 2016 us=539802 ++ Certificate has EKU (str) TLS Web Server Authentication, expects TLS Web
 Server Authentication
Sun Aug 14 08:33:32 2016 us=539806 VERIFY EKU OK
Sun Aug 14 08:33:32 2016 us=539809 VERIFY OK: depth=0, C=US, ST=Minnesota, O=Trouble Shooting OpenVPN, CN=tsho
ot-server, emailAddress=ecrist@secure-computing.net
Sun Aug 14 08:33:32 2016 us=559323 Data Channel Encrypt: Cipher 'BF-CBC' initialized with 128 bit key
Sun Aug 14 08:33:32 2016 us=559345 Data Channel Encrypt: Using 160 bit message hash 'SHA1' for HMAC authentica
tion
Sun Aug 14 08:33:32 2016 us=559392 Data Channel Decrypt: Cipher 'BF-CBC' initialized with 128 bit key
Sun Aug 14 08:33:32 2016 us=559399 Data Channel Decrypt: Using 160 bit message hash 'SHA1' for HMAC authentica
tion
Sun Aug 14 08:33:32 2016 us=559429 Control Channel: TLSv1.2, cipher TLSv1/SSLv3 DHE-RSA-AES256-GCM-SHA384, 102
4 bit RSA
Sun Aug 14 08:33:32 2016 us=559446 [tshoot-server] Peer Connection Initiated with [AF_INET]192.168.19.37:1194
Sun Aug 14 08:33:34 2016 us=725207 SENT CONTROL [tshoot-server]: 'PUSH_REQUEST' (status=1)
Sun Aug 14 08:33:34 2016 us=726842 PUSH: Received control message: 'PUSH_REPLY,route-gateway 192.168.80.1,topo
logy subnet,ping 10,ping-restart 60,ifconfig 192.168.80.2 255.255.255.0'
Sun Aug 14 08:33:34 2016 us=726919 OPTIONS IMPORT: timers and/or timeouts modified
Sun Aug 14 08:33:34 2016 us=726929 OPTIONS IMPORT: --ifconfig/up options modified
Sun Aug 14 08:33:34 2016 us=726936 OPTIONS IMPORT: route-related options modified
Sun Aug 14 08:33:34 2016 us=727264 Opened utun device utun0
Sun Aug 14 08:33:34 2016 us=727297 do_ifconfig, tt->ipv6=0, tt->did_ifconfig_ipv6_setup=0
Sun Aug 14 08:33:34 2016 us=727337 /sbin/ifconfig utun0 delete
ifconfig: ioctl (SIOCDIFADDR): Can't assign requested address
Sun Aug 14 08:33:34 2016 us=732894 NOTE: Tried to delete pre-existing tun/tap instance -- No Problem if failur
e
Sun Aug 14 08:33:34 2016 us=732948 /sbin/ifconfig utun0 192.168.80.2 192.168.80.2 netmask 255.255.255.0 mtu 15
00 up
Sun Aug 14 08:33:34 2016 us=734969 /sbin/route add -net 192.168.80.0 192.168.80.2 255.255.255.0
```

Valid EKU applied to the server certificate

The screenshot here shows a server without the server EKU applied to the certificate. In this case, there is a cascading list of TLS errors displayed following the failed EKU verification. These occur due to the tear-down of the TLS exchange once an error is discovered.

These samples are from the view of the OpenVPN client. Similar messages will be present when the server is expecting the client certificates define the EKU for client:

```
                                    author@client
Sun Aug 14 08:34:36 2016 us=47916   port_share_host = '[UNDEF]'
Sun Aug 14 08:34:36 2016 us=47992   port_share_port = 0
Sun Aug 14 08:34:36 2016 us=48009   client = ENABLED
Sun Aug 14 08:34:36 2016 us=48013   pull = ENABLED
Sun Aug 14 08:34:36 2016 us=48018   auth_user_pass_file = '[UNDEF]'
Sun Aug 14 08:34:36 2016 us=48023 OpenVPN 2.3.11 x86_64-apple-darwin [SSL (OpenSSL)] [LZO] [PKCS11] [MH] [IPv6
] built on Jul 18 2016
Sun Aug 14 08:34:36 2016 us=48031 library versions: OpenSSL 1.0.2h  3 May 2016, LZO 2.09
Sun Aug 14 08:34:36 2016 us=48730 Control Channel MTU parms [ L:1541 D:1212 EF:38 EB:0 ET:0 EL:3 ]
Sun Aug 14 08:34:36 2016 us=48789 Socket Buffers: R=[196724->196724] S=[9216->9216]
Sun Aug 14 08:34:36 2016 us=49069 Data Channel MTU parms [ L:1541 D:1450 EF:41 EB:12 ET:0 EL:3 ]
Sun Aug 14 08:34:36 2016 us=49099 Local Options String: 'V4,dev-type tun,link-mtu 1541,tun-mtu 1500,proto UDPv
4,cipher BF-CBC,auth SHA1,keysize 128,key-method 2,tls-client'
Sun Aug 14 08:34:36 2016 us=49117 Expected Remote Options String: 'V4,dev-type tun,link-mtu 1541,tun-mtu 1500,
proto UDPv4,cipher BF-CBC,auth SHA1,keysize 128,key-method 2,tls-server'
Sun Aug 14 08:34:36 2016 us=49126 Local Options hash (VER=V4): '3514370b'
Sun Aug 14 08:34:36 2016 us=49132 Expected Remote Options hash (VER=V4): '239669a8'
Sun Aug 14 08:34:36 2016 us=49143 UDPv4 link local (bound): [undef]
Sun Aug 14 08:34:36 2016 us=49148 UDPv4 link remote: [AF_INET]192.168.19.37:1194
Sun Aug 14 08:34:36 2016 us=51775 TLS: Initial packet from [AF_INET]192.168.19.37:1194, sid=0a1431d6 301a793c
Sun Aug 14 08:34:36 2016 us=56336 VERIFY OK: depth=1, C=US, ST=Minnesota, L=St Paul, O=Trouble Shooting OpenVP
N, CN=Trouble Shooting OpenVPN, emailAddress=ecrist@secure-computing.net
Sun Aug 14 08:34:36 2016 us=56498 Certificate does not have key usage extension
Sun Aug 14 08:34:36 2016 us=56507 VERIFY KU ERROR
Sun Aug 14 08:34:36 2016 us=56564 OpenSSL: error:14090086:SSL routines:ssl3_get_server_certificate:certificate
 verify failed
Sun Aug 14 08:34:36 2016 us=56571 TLS_ERROR: BIO read tls_read_plaintext error
Sun Aug 14 08:34:36 2016 us=56575 TLS Error: TLS object -> incoming plaintext read error
Sun Aug 14 08:34:36 2016 us=56579 TLS Error: TLS handshake failed
Sun Aug 14 08:34:36 2016 us=56690 TCP/UDP: Closing socket
Sun Aug 14 08:34:36 2016 us=56752 SIGUSR1[soft,tls-error] received, process restarting
Sun Aug 14 08:34:36 2016 us=56761 Restart pause, 2 second(s)
^CSun Aug 14 08:34:37 2016 us=539931 SIGINT[hard,init_instance] received, process exiting
author@client:~-> 
```

Summary

OpenVPN has powerful logging capability suited well for the end user, the system administrator, and the software developer. Detailed information can be displayed from high-level networking and configuration options down to very low-level cryptographic components information.

Understanding the log file and the various affirmative and warning messages allows you to quickly and reliably determine the cause of a fault or to confirm a working setup. There are still some configuration parameters in which errors will not be apparent within the log file, and those will be covered in later chapters.

5
Client and Server Startup

As illustrated in Chapter 4, *The Log File*, many of problems with OpenVPN arise during the server or client startup procedure. These problems can involve networking, virtual network adapters, and differing configuration options between the two endpoints. This chapter will bring to light the common sources of startup problems and identify the fixes for those.

Some network configuration will be addressed, but Chapter 7, *Network and Routing*, will have a comprehensive explanation of network troubleshooting and core network and routing concepts.

File and process permissions

For OpenVPN to be effective, the user running the OpenVPN process will need to have the necessary privileges and access to the system, networking, and filesystem. This includes access to writing log files, modifying network adapter settings and the system routing tables, and executing scripts or programs.

Privilege de-escalation

As stated earlier, to make many of the network and routing changes, OpenVPN will need some initial privileges in excess of a typical user. Once these changes have been made, there is usually no need to retain these administrative rights. Using the --user and --group configuration parameters, the administrator can instruct OpenVPN that unprivileged user to operate as once the initialization process has completed.

There are caveats to dropping to an unprivileged user, however. First, all files that the OpenVPN process needs to use during normal operation must be readable and/or writable by the unprivileged user. This includes `--client-config-directory` and the files within, and any `connect` or `disconnect` scripts.

The permissions of the **Certificate Revocation List** (**CRL**) is an easy one to forget, with the certificate key being a close second. There is a configuration option (`--persist-key`), which keeps the key resident in memory, preventing the process from having to re-read the file from disk during `SIGUSR1` or restart caused by `--ping-restart`.

In the following screenshot, all files are owned by the user `nobody` and the group `nobody`, except the `tshoot-server.key` file, which is still owned by the user `root` and the group `wheel`:

```
● ● ●                                    author@server
author@server:/usr/local/etc/openvpn-> ls -lh
total 48
-rw-r--r--  1 root    nobody   1.4K Aug  1 12:03 ca.crt
drwxr-xr-x  2 root    nobody   512B Nov 25 04:00 ccd
-rw-r--r--  1 root    nobody   245B Aug  1 12:09 dh1024.pem
-rw-r--r--  1 root    nobody   305B Aug 14 01:25 openvpn-noeku.conf
-rw-r--r--  1 root    nobody   342B Dec 17 22:06 openvpn.conf
-rw-r--r--  1 root    nobody   344B Dec 17 22:07 openvpn2.conf
drwxr-xr-x  2 root    nobody   512B Dec 17 09:54 tmp
-rw-r--r--  1 root    nobody   4.0K Aug  1 12:04 tshoot-server.crt
-rw-------  1 root    wheel    916B Aug  1 12:04 tshoot-server.key
-rw-r--r--  1 root    nobody   4.0K Aug  1 12:04 tshoot-server.pem
author@server:/usr/local/etc/openvpn->
```

A key file owned by root : wheel, inaccessible to the "nobody" user

If we were to apply the `--user nobody` and `--group nobody` options, a soft restart of the server would fail because the key is unreadable.

Networking privileges

Changes to the system routing tables, adding IP addresses to interfaces, and changing the state of network interfaces typically require root or administrative privileges.

Port assignment and use

As a general rule, processes attempting to bind to TCP or UDP ports below `1024` require root permission. This prevents a normal, unprivileged user, from standing a daemon up on a port where a common system process normally runs and mimicking an official process.

For example, on a server where SSH was not running, without this privileged port check, a user could start their own SSH daemon that was customized (or *compromised*) in some way to sniff or track user credentials or session traffic. An administrator could unwittingly connect to the SSH daemon, log in, and run system commands.

In November, 2004, the **Internet Assigned Numbers Authority** (**IANA**) reserved port `1194` for OpenVPN, for both the TCP and UDP protocols. Prior to this assignment, OpenVPN defaulted to using port `5000`; OpenVPN 2.0-beta17 and later default to the IANA assigned port. With the new and old ports, OpenVPN falls outside the lower `1024` privileged port reservation, making the root requirement at this stage moot. It is required for other parts, which are described later.

It is possible to override the default port by specifying the `--port` option in the OpenVPN server or client configuration. The port used locally and remotely is expected to be the same unless the `--lport` and `--rport` options are used. These should be mirror images of each other if used and only apply to a static key setup; OpenVPN will use a dynamic (random) outbound port from a client with `--tls-client` is used.

Multiple daemons

If multiple OpenVPN process is going to be used, the listen address of each must be different. If you attempt to start another OpenVPN process using a port that is already in use, an error will appear in the logs. In addition, all the major operating systems provide a utility named `netstat` to help identify what ports are in use on your system. The exact syntax varies across Windows, BSD, and Linux, but the command name is the same on all three.

To demonstrate its use, the following screenshot shows the first page of output on Windows 7:

```
Active Connections

  Proto  Local Address          Foreign Address        State
  TCP    0.0.0.0:80             winblows7:0            LISTENING
  TCP    0.0.0.0:135            winblows7:0            LISTENING
  TCP    0.0.0.0:445            winblows7:0            LISTENING
  TCP    0.0.0.0:515            winblows7:0            LISTENING
  TCP    0.0.0.0:554            winblows7:0            LISTENING
  TCP    0.0.0.0:1025           winblows7:0            LISTENING
  TCP    0.0.0.0:1026           winblows7:0            LISTENING
  TCP    0.0.0.0:1027           winblows7:0            LISTENING
  TCP    0.0.0.0:1038           winblows7:0            LISTENING
  TCP    0.0.0.0:1039           winblows7:0            LISTENING
  TCP    0.0.0.0:1040           winblows7:0            LISTENING
  TCP    0.0.0.0:2869           winblows7:0            LISTENING
  TCP    0.0.0.0:3390           winblows7:0            LISTENING
  TCP    0.0.0.0:4242           winblows7:0            LISTENING
  TCP    0.0.0.0:5357           winblows7:0            LISTENING
  TCP    0.0.0.0:5800           winblows7:0            LISTENING
  TCP    0.0.0.0:5900           winblows7:0            LISTENING
  TCP    0.0.0.0:8019           winblows7:0            LISTENING
-- More  --
```

The output of netstat -a on Windows 7

This system has an IIS 7 server running, which shows up as the first entry in the table. The command I used for this was:

```
netstat -a | more
```

The address of `0.0.0.0` denotes that the entry is valid for all IPs on the system and `:80` that follows is the port number (the `www` port). The `State` column indicates the system as `LISTENING`. This is used to identify services that are awaiting a connection.

If we were to scroll further down in the output, active connections (whether inbound or outbound) will be denoted with the state `ESTABLISHED`. If `cmd.exe` is executed with administrative privileges, you can add the `-b` and `-o` options to `netstat` and it will display the process name and process ID (the `PID` column). Note that IIS does not show the `W3P.exe` process name as a security precaution; however, you can see other example process names:

```
Active Connections

  Proto  Local Address           Foreign Address        State          PID
  TCP    0.0.0.0:80              winblows7:0            LISTENING      4
Can not obtain ownership information
  TCP    0.0.0.0:135             winblows7:0            LISTENING      720
  RpcSs
[svchost.exe]
  TCP    0.0.0.0:445             winblows7:0            LISTENING      4
Can not obtain ownership information
  TCP    0.0.0.0:515             winblows7:0            LISTENING      1496
[cenlpd.exe]
  TCP    0.0.0.0:554             winblows7:0            LISTENING      4580
[wmpnetwk.exe]
  TCP    0.0.0.0:1025            winblows7:0            LISTENING      380
[wininit.exe]
  TCP    0.0.0.0:1026            winblows7:0            LISTENING      800
  eventlog
[svchost.exe]
  TCP    0.0.0.0:1027            winblows7:0            LISTENING      932
  Schedule
-- More  --
```

netstat -a on run with elevated privileges

Adapter and routing table changes

Making changes to the networking configuration and system network interfaces almost always requires administrator or root permissions. For interactive user sessions, there are utilities such as sudo that allow temporary one-off escalation of privileges. This can be tedious to maintain and difficult to implement for an application such as OpenVPN that provides no mechanism in order to instruct it to leverage sudo outside the scripted components.

Another more recent advent is polkit, which allows the Linux administrator to instruct the system that certain users or groups of users can perform specific actions. polkit can be used to provide a normal user to make interface and routing table changes.

Chroot

An established concept on UNIX and Linux systems is a **chroot** environment. This environment segregates a process or set of processes from the rest of the system by setting a new root path. Both the causes of problems with chroot, as well as the benefit of using it are the same: the process can only access files that reside within this new root path.

From a command line, you can run any command within a chroot environment by simply running the `chroot` command. To use this environment with OpenVPN, the similarly named `--chroot` option is provided. When this option is used, everything needed must reside within this `chroot` path, including any dependent commands and files. Some examples include the following:

- `--client-connect` and `--client-disconnect` script files
- OpenVPN certificates and keys
- On the server, the CRL file
- `--client-config-dir`

The following screenshot shows what happens when we attempt to simply add the `--chroot` directive to our known working configuration file. In this case, we defined our `chroot` environment as `/usr/local/etc/openvpn/`, which has the default configuration location on FreeBSD for OpenVPN. The immediate failures are the pathing to our CRL and a valid temporary directory:

```
author@server:/usr/local/etc/openvpn-> cat openvpn.conf
dh dh1024.pem
dev tun
server 192.168.80.0 255.255.255.0
ca ca.crt
cert tshoot-server.crt
key tshoot-server.key
topology subnet
status /var/log/openvpn-status.log 5
keepalive 10 60
crl-verify /usr/local/etc/ssl-admin/prog/crl.pem
#log-append /var/log/openvpn.log
verb 4
proto udp
port 1194
client-config-dir ccd
chroot /usr/local/etc/openvpn/
author@server:/usr/local/etc/openvpn-> openvpn --config openvpn.conf
Options error: --crl-verify fails with '/usr/local/etc/openvpn///usr/local/etc/ssl-admin/prog/crl.pem': No such file or
directory
Options error: Temporary directory (--tmp-dir) fails with '/usr/local/etc/openvpn///tmp': No such file or directory
Options error: Please correct these errors.
Use --help for more information.
author@server:/usr/local/etc/openvpn-> █
```

Failed startup with –chroot due to incorrect relative paths

Even if we fix these errors by removing the line to our CRL and creating the `tmp` directory in `/usr/local/etc/openvpn`, there will be additional errors, at the very least at shutdown. Without dependent programs, such as `/sbin/ifconfig`, destroying the interface fails.

Any other commands will need to be copied in to the chroot environment with correct pathing. With a well-built environment, you will end up with a directory that mimics a normal root file system.

Writing to log files will continue to work since the file descriptor is opened prior to the `chroot` command. This makes it possible to put the log and status file outside the chroot environment.

```
author@server:/usr/local/etc/openvpn-> tail /var/log/openvpn.log
Sat Dec 17 09:58:24 2016 us=122077 UDPv4 link remote: [undef]
Sat Dec 17 09:58:24 2016 us=122086 MULTI: multi_init called, r=256 v=256
Sat Dec 17 09:58:24 2016 us=122107 IFCONFIG POOL: base=192.168.80.2 size=252, ipv6=0
Sat Dec 17 09:58:24 2016 us=122123 Initialization Sequence Completed
Sat Dec 17 09:58:27 2016 us=476016 event_wait : Interrupted system call (code=4)
Sat Dec 17 09:58:27 2016 us=476150 TCP/UDP: Closing socket
Sat Dec 17 09:58:27 2016 us=476176 Closing TUN/TAP interface
Sat Dec 17 09:58:27 2016 us=476276 /sbin/ifconfig tun0 destroy
Sat Dec 17 09:58:27 2016 us=476606 FreeBSD 'destroy tun interface' failed (non-critical): could not execute external program
Sat Dec 17 09:58:27 2016 us=476641 SIGINT[hard,] received, process exiting
author@server:/usr/local/etc/openvpn-> 
```

Missing ifconfig command causes failed interface shutdown

There are additional caveats to these restricted environments that are outside the scope of this book. Varying operating systems handle device files differently, and commands such as `ifconfig` will require access to the device in a known location. Some make this easy by allowing you to mount the `/dev` filesystem within the chroot environment, others may not.

The key to remember here is that everything you intend to manipulate (files, interfaces, commands, scripts, and so on) must reside within the scope of the `chroot` path. You can test this most easily by putting yourself in that environment and attempting to execute the same commands.

This can be a hairy path, too, as you can see later. In addition to many of the executables, you will find various shared libraries are missing that must be copied in to the environment:

```
author@server:/usr/local/etc/openvpn-> chroot /usr/local/etc/openvpn/ /sbin/ifconfig
chroot: /sbin/ifconfig: No such file or directory
author@server:/usr/local/etc/openvpn-> mkdir sbin
author@server:/usr/local/etc/openvpn-> cp /sbin/ifconfig sbin/
author@server:/usr/local/etc/openvpn-> chroot /usr/local/etc/openvpn/ /sbin/ifconfig
Shared object "libbsdxml.so.4" not found, required by "ifconfig"
author@server:/usr/local/etc/openvpn-> locate libbsdxml.so.4
/lib/libbsdxml.so.4
/usr/lib32/libbsdxml.so.4
author@server:/usr/local/etc/openvpn-> mkdir lib
author@server:/usr/local/etc/openvpn-> cp /lib/libbsdxml.so.4 lib
author@server:/usr/local/etc/openvpn-> chroot /usr/local/etc/openvpn/ /sbin/ifconfig
Shared object "libsbuf.so.6" not found, required by "ifconfig"
author@server:/usr/local/etc/openvpn-> ▊
```

Assorted shared libraries/objects may be required, depending on the utility run inside the chroot environment

Scripting

For many years, I worked for a small company and most projects where completed in an ad hoc manner. We identified a problem and went straight away to writing a script or making a software change.

A few years ago, I obtained a systems engineering role for a much larger organization. At the new company, there was a much more formal software development environment that included an exhaustive process:

1. A problem report must be filed, indicating the specific bug or feature needing work. Many times, it might be the developer him/herself entering the issue in the database.

2. The issue is discussed in the next team meeting at what is named an **Software Change Control Board** (**SCCB**). This team, consisting of many stakeholders, dispositions each issue and determines whether it is accepted for work.

3. Once an issue is accepted, any requirements changes or additions is considered. The software requirements help drive formal software testing and acceptance later.

4. The issue and the requirement is assigned to the developer doing the work. Any changes related to the initial issue or bug are made.

5. The software changes are routed to a code review system where managers and senior developers can comment, reject, or ultimately accept the changes for commit.

6. Automated and manual tests are written against the requirement that was changed or created. These tend to be strict and literal to the wording of the requirement. For example, a requirement that reads:

   Username shall contain alphanumeric characters from letter a through letter z and number 0 through 9.

   This will specifically also exclude anything else.

7. Finally, the tests are executed against the software and further changes to either meet requirements or changes to requirements to more closely match software needs are made.

   Rinse and repeat.

Many corporate development teams follow a similar model, and increasing numbers of open source software development teams are, as well. The OpenVPN team also follows a similar development cycle, though not quite as formal.

The most important part of this cycle, from a smaller scope, is the requirement definition. I find it is much easier to contain my scripting to a given task if I take some time, even a small amount, to define what, exactly, I expect from the program once complete.

Defining a requirement or set of requirements, for an OpenVPN script can not only help with writing the code to do what is necessary, but will ultimately aid in troubleshooting, either during development or when problems occur later.

Up and down scripts

There are many moving parts with client- and server-side `--up` scripts. The server side tends to be relatively static, and there is only a single configuration. Client side, however, there are as many different configurations as there are unique client computers.

Because of these differences, assumptions made within a client-side script may be incorrect. These may include virtual adapter device names, local network addresses and routing, and commands. Also, the scripts written for a Windows client will not function correctly on a Linux system and vice versa.

In my experience, if the start up script is working, it is relatively simple to apply the same logic, in reverse, to create a working `--down` script. All the permission, pathing, and naming idiosyncrasies will be hashed out during development of the start up routine.

During development and troubleshooting, I find it is easiest to start an OpenVPN process, and include some debugging messages in the `--up` or `--down` script. For the first test, we can use the following script:

```
#!/bin/sh

# Test OpenVPN --up script

set -x
exec 2>&1
printenv > /tmp/ovpn-env.$$

logger -p local3.notice -t LOGTEST "Hello world! From: `whoami`"
```

This will add a simple log entry in `/var/log/messages` with text such as:

Dec 25 10:23:09 tshoot-srvr LOGTEST: Hello world! From: nobody

The three highlighted lines are excellent to debug scripts. The first line will cause each executed statement to print in the OpenVPN log file. This shows variable expansion and actual command use, helping identify errors in variable names and command pathing.

The second highlighted line will cause both `STDERR` and `STDOUT` to output the same, showing error output that may be hidden from the log file.

Finally, the third highlighted line will cause it to print out the entire environment variable list and their values to a file at `/tmp/ovpn-env.<PID>` where `<PID>` is replaced with the script process ID. This is useful when debugging, so you can ensure the values you are receiving are what you are expecting.

I've saved this file as `/usr/local/etc/openvpn/up.sh` and set it to be executable by everyone, and I've added the `--up up.sh` parameter to our `openvpn.conf` file. The user name printed after `From:` will be the effective user running the OpenVPN process.

Our first attempt at running OpenVPN shows a serious error; I've forgotten to add the `--script-security` option to the configuration, which would allow the execution of external scripts. I've highlighted the errors in the following screenshot:

```
Sun Dec 25 10:27:09 2016 us=681849    cf_max = 0
Sun Dec 25 10:27:09 2016 us=681852    cf_per = 0
Sun Dec 25 10:27:09 2016 us=681864    max_clients = 1024
Sun Dec 25 10:27:09 2016 us=681867    max_routes_per_client = 256
Sun Dec 25 10:27:09 2016 us=681870    auth_user_pass_verify_script = '[UNDEF]'
Sun Dec 25 10:27:09 2016 us=681873    auth_user_pass_verify_script_via_file = DISABLED
Sun Dec 25 10:27:09 2016 us=681876    port_share_host = '[UNDEF]'
Sun Dec 25 10:27:09 2016 us=681879    port_share_port = 0
Sun Dec 25 10:27:09 2016 us=681881    client = DISABLED
Sun Dec 25 10:27:09 2016 us=681902    pull = DISABLED
Sun Dec 25 10:27:09 2016 us=681905    auth_user_pass_file = '[UNDEF]'
Sun Dec 25 10:27:09 2016 us=681909 OpenVPN 2.3.11 amd64-portbld-freebsd10.1 [SSL (OpenSSL)] [LZO] [MH] [I
Pv6] built on Jul 26 2016
Sun Dec 25 10:27:09 2016 us=681916 library versions: OpenSSL 1.0.1j-freebsd 15 Oct 2014, LZO 2.09
Sun Dec 25 10:27:09 2016 us=682002 NOTE: starting with OpenVPN 2.1, '--script-security 2' or higher is re
quired to call user-defined scripts or executables
Sun Dec 25 10:27:09 2016 us=682716 Diffie-Hellman initialized with 1024 bit key
Sun Dec 25 10:27:09 2016 us=683103 TLS-Auth MTU parms [ L:1541 D:1212 EF:38 EB:0 ET:0 EL:3 ]
Sun Dec 25 10:27:09 2016 us=683121 Socket Buffers: R=[42080->42080] S=[9216->9216]
Sun Dec 25 10:27:09 2016 us=683203 TUN/TAP device /dev/tun0 opened
Sun Dec 25 10:27:09 2016 us=683217 do_ifconfig, tt->ipv6=0, tt->did_ifconfig_ipv6_setup=0
Sun Dec 25 10:27:09 2016 us=683233 /sbin/ifconfig tun0 192.168.80.1 192.168.80.2 mtu 1500 netmask 255.255
.255.0 up
Sun Dec 25 10:27:09 2016 us=684340 /sbin/route add -net 192.168.80.0 192.168.80.1 255.255.255.0
add net 192.168.80.0: gateway 192.168.80.1
Sun Dec 25 10:27:09 2016 us=684921 up.sh tun0 1500 1541 192.168.80.1 255.255.255.0 init
Sun Dec 25 10:27:09 2016 us=684950 WARNING: External program may not be called unless '--script-security
2' or higher is enabled. See --help text or man page for detailed info.
Sun Dec 25 10:27:09 2016 us=684968 WARNING: Failed running command (--up/--down): external program fork f
ailed
Sun Dec 25 10:27:09 2016 us=684982 Exiting due to fatal error
author@server:/usr/local/etc/openvpn-> 
```

The execution of the –up script fails due to missing –script-security parameter

Once the `--script-security 2` setting is defined, the VPN is initialized, and I can see the
log entry in `/var/log/messages`. Note that both my test log entry, when I ran as user
`nobody`, as well as the entry from `root` are displayed here:

```
Sun Dec 25 10:37:37 2016 us=491906 Initialization Sequence Completed
^CSun Dec 25 10:37:53 2016 us=343531 event_wait : Interrupted system call (code=4)
Sun Dec 25 10:37:53 2016 us=343685 TCP/UDP: Closing socket
Sun Dec 25 10:37:53 2016 us=343717 Closing TUN/TAP interface
Sun Dec 25 10:37:53 2016 us=343873 /sbin/ifconfig tun0 destroy
Sun Dec 25 10:37:53 2016 us=345149 SIGINT[hard,] received, process exiting
author@server:/usr/local/etc/openvpn-> grep LOGTEST /var/log/messages
Dec 25 10:23:09 tshoot-srvr LOGTEST: Hello world! From: nobody
Dec 25 10:37:37 tshoot-srvr LOGTEST: Hello world! From: root
author@server:/usr/local/etc/openvpn-> 
```

Log entries appear from the execution of the –up script

Now, to extend our script a bit, we can show the context in which it is being executed. You'll notice in the first screenshot at our `--up` script attempt, the first line of the highlighted content shows our script being executed, along with a series of parameters. You can use these parameters in your script to change the script behavior in addition to a list of environment variables. We can use `$script_type` to change the output of our log message:

```
#!/bin/sh

# Test OpenVPN combined --up/--down script

# this should just added a log entry in /var/log/messages

logger -p local3.notice -t LOGTEST "OpenVPN running as
`whoami` for $script_type script."
```

I've added `--down up.sh` to the `openvpn.conf` file. Running a quick startup and shutdown of OpenVPN again, we can now see that our updated message shows up for both `--up` and `--down`:

```
Sun Dec 25 10:52:29 2016 us=44363 Closing TUN/TAP interface
Sun Dec 25 10:52:29 2016 us=44519 /sbin/ifconfig tun0 destroy
Sun Dec 25 10:52:29 2016 us=45878 up.sh tun0 1500 1541 192.168.80.1 255.255.255.0 init
Sun Dec 25 10:52:29 2016 us=47642 SIGINT[hard,] received, process exiting
author@server:/usr/local/etc/openvpn-> grep LOGTEST /var/log/messages
Dec 25 10:23:09 tshoot-srvr LOGTEST: Hello world! From: nobody
Dec 25 10:37:37 tshoot-srvr LOGTEST: Hello world! From: root
Dec 25 10:45:34 tshoot-srvr LOGTEST: Hello world! From: root
Dec 25 10:45:47 tshoot-srvr LOGTEST: Hello world! From: root
Dec 25 10:46:18 tshoot-srvr LOGTEST: Hello world! From: root
Dec 25 10:46:22 tshoot-srvr LOGTEST: Hello world! From: root
Dec 25 10:52:24 tshoot-srvr LOGTEST: OpenVPN running as root for up script.
Dec 25 10:52:29 tshoot-srvr LOGTEST: OpenVPN running as root for down script.
author@server:/usr/local/etc/openvpn-> 
```

Log message changes for $script_type environment variable

Connect and disconnect scripts

The `--client-connect` and `--client-disconnect` scripts are very similar to the `--up` and `--down` scripts, but are only used on the server side. These scripts are typically used for logging, reporting, or local configuration that is unique to a given client. Troubleshooting these is all but impossible if you are a client on a remote OpenVPN server unless you have direct server access.

The `connect` script is capable of authorization and route assignments, and it could be suspected if a client is having some odd connectivity issues.

UDP troubleshooting

As a general rule, UDP is a better option for VPN traffic than TCP. TCP works very hard to ensure that every single packet makes it across the wire (or any other medium) uncorrupted and in order. For some things, such as SSH, file transfers, and web traffic, this is a good thing; we expect the resulting content to be legible and generally in its original form.

When connectivity is reliable with relatively little packet loss, TCP can function just fine for VPN. When that link drops packets and becomes unreliable, the problem can be amplified dramatically when the encapsulated traffic is also using TCP. The resulting traffic includes retransmit from both the OpenVPN processes at either end and the encapsulated traffic at both ends. This results in potentially four times the packet count.

By its nature, UDP is a connectionless protocol. UDP is great for data where it is acceptable to receive packets out of order or when packets can go missing. The out-of-order packets are typically discarded since the application has likely already moved on to processing the later packets and processing earlier packets would be disruptive.

Voice over Internet Protocol (VoIP) is one good example of this scenario. In a voice or video conversation with someone, we are listening and/or viewing the conversation in real time. It would be undesirable to hear words or see facial expression out of order. The conversation quickly would become incomprehensible; it is much preferable to simply ignore a dropped consonant or see a short hang in the video stream. On a smaller scale, rendering a portion of a frame or part of a word that is a second or more old is of little use.

Traffic across a VPN is similar. The encapsulated traffic is already going to be engineered to handle either transmission assurance (TCP) or packet loss and delay in a graceful manner. So, using UDP for the overall VPN traffic, we allow the application transiting the VPN to handle any connection quality issues.

 Sometimes using TCP for a VPN tunnel is unavoidable, but do so if you can. The community support staff often references two links for why TCP within TCP is a bad idea:
`http://sites.inka.de/~bigred/devel/tcp-tcp.html` and
`http://www.openvpn.net/papers/BLUG-talk/14.html`.

Because of this *connectionless* state of a UDP tunnel, neither the client or server truly know when the link to the other end has gone away or failed. To help deal with lost connections, OpenVPN has the `--ping` and `--ping-restart` options.

If you are using UDP for your OpenVPN tunnel and traffic periodically stops working, adding the `--ping-restart` option will help OpenVPN detect connection failures and reconnect the tunnel to a useful state.

UDP and firewalls

Because UDP is connectionless, another hurdle for this traffic is the border firewall. Some firewalls will attempt to perform a fake *keep-state* on the traffic pattern with some level of default timeout when no further traffic witnessed.

Using the `--ping` option, OpenVPN will spend periodic ping packets across VPN to the remote endpoint to keep these fake *keep-state* sessions active. Without this, the firewall may determine no further traffic is expected and shut down the session. This will not prevent traffic from leaving the firewall, but will block the other side from talking in to that endpoint.

This can potentially happen for either side, but it is typically a client-side problem. The server side will normally have an explicit rule in the firewall that allows the inbound UDP traffic, whereas the client side uses a random high-numbered port.

If the client is having connection problems, there may be a large delay on the server side before that system is listed as disconnected. This will delay updates to things such as the `--status` log or the execution of `--client-disconnect`. There is a client-side option available named `--explicit-exit-notify`, which will cause the client system to notify the remote OpenVPN server that it is exiting.

Summary

This chapter was much less about what an administrator can do to fix a problem and more about identifying specific causes of a given problem. Some possibly new tools, such as `netstat`, were introduced. Permissions at multiple levels were also examined, from process level to the filesystem.

6
Certificates and Authentication

There are many methods of authentication available within OpenVPN. At its introduction, OpenVPN supported only a simple pre-shared key but today supports X.509 certificate chains, user and password authentication, and third-party authentication plugins and scripts. Each of these can be used separately, or they can be combined to form a robust authentication and authorization framework.

Along with robustness, complexity creates potential confusion and adds difficulty in troubleshooting authentication issues, understanding how the individual components affect the connection process and where logic is applied in accepting or rejecting a client or user.

Mismanagement of your PKI can have great consequences, whether your PKI is relatively local in scope (a single organization or hobbyist's systems), or global, such as a public **certificate authority** (**CA**) providing certificates to customers. There were two cases in 2016 of trusted CAs that lost trust with various web browser vendors. Both WoSign and StartCom lost Apple's (Safari) trust as of September 30, 2016, and Mozilla (Firefox) and Google (Chrome) as of October 21, 2016. This was due to poor signing practices and poor key management.

 You can read more about these events at eWeek (http://www.eweek.com/security/why-browser-vendors-chose-to-dist rust-2-certificate-authorities.html) or at The Register (http://www.theregister.co.uk/2016/11/02/google_punts_wosign_sta rtcom_from_good_guy_certificate_club/).

File permissions

Best practice often dictates that once operations requiring escalated privileges have been completed, a daemon or process should drop to an unprivileged user. Many of the OpenVPN *how-to* documents illustrate this by calling the --user and --group configuration parameters. These same instructions, along with other guidance suggest that your configuration, certificates, keys, and other related files have root ownership. This practice prevents an unprivileged user or process from surreptitiously changing keys, routes, and other parameters.

Once OpenVPN reduces its running privileges, it will be unable to re-read the configuration files, certificates, and keys without some additional options. This may be the desired behavior, and it is the more secure configuration though it is not very resilient. When an option such as --ping-restart is used, the OpenVPN process will attempt to restart itself, requiring a re-read of the certificate, keys, and configuration. If privileges have been dropped to a user that does not have read access to these files or paths, the restart will fail and OpenVPN will exit.

To accommodate this scenario, there are a pair of options that allow the OpenVPN process to reuse or retain data that was read before privileges were dropped. The --persist-tun option instructs OpenVPN to reuse the existing tun or tap device and to not re-execute the --up or --down scripts. Without this option, the process would require special permissions within the operating system to modify or change the virtual network adapter, its settings, and routing. Finally, the --persist-key option instructs OpenVPN not to re-read key files during SIGUSR1 or --ping-restart.

Be certain to always protect your certificate key files. Although it may be a minor inconvenience to configure OpenVPN to execute and operate as an unprivileged user, there is great benefit in the long run. Certificates are shared clear, over the wire, and the public portion of the exchange. If your private keys become available or are easy to read, a client or other (OpenVPN, LDAP, mail, and so on) server could potentially be impersonated. If your CA key is exposed, there is potential for rogue-signed certificates that your existing systems would trust.

Pre-shared keys

Using **pre-shared key** (**PSK**) is where OpenVPN started. The *static key how-to* on the OpenVPN website is often the first place aspiring VPN administrators begin. Problems with PSKs are relatively easy to identify as the VPN will simply fail to operate.

There are two scenarios where PSKs are used, in a static key point-to-point VPN and with the `--tls-auth` directive in the more commonly deployed client-server topology. This section will specifically cover the prior, static key, scenario. The latter, the `--tls-auth` scenario, is specifically covered in depth in `Chapter 7`, *Network and Routing*. The advice listed there equally applies to VPNs using PSKs for the data channel, as well. Pay close attention to `--key-direction`, if used.

Certificate authentication

Since the release of OpenVPN 2.x, certificate authentication has been the most prolific deployment of OpenVPN in the wild. The earlier static key only supported two remote endpoints, neither really being a client nor a server. This is not useful when more than a single remote client is desired.

Certificate chain overview

X.509 is a notable standard for **Public Key Infrastructure** (**PKI**), defining a hierarchical topology of CAs and their signed child certificates. The general concept is that, at that root of the chain, is an authority certificate, the CA. This CA certificate can be used to sign child certificates. Anyone (or thing, system, and so on) that trusts the root, inherently trusts the child certificates.

CA has the ability to sign child certificates with varying capabilities. Some will have differing key usage or KU; others might have subordinate CA rights. With cascading trust, subordinate CAs are generally given the same trust as their parent CA in a given trust store.

The screenshot given later shows the certificate chain for the OpenVPN community web server. In this case, there is a parent CA certificate, **Go Daddy Root Certificate Authority – G2**, a subordinate CA certificate, **Go Daddy Secure Certificate Authority – G2**, and the OpenVPN wildcard certificate, ***.openvpn.net**.

The chain of trust starts from the presented server or client certificate, in our case, the ***.openvpn.net** certificate. In this example, the Safari web browser is the client agent, and it will look up the certificate chain in the local trust store based on the information and additional certificates presented by the web server. If Safari and my Mac have the subordinate CA in the key store, trust will be dispositioned based on the settings within that trust store. In our example here, **Go Daddy Root Certificate Authority – G2** is present and trusted in the local certificate store. The web server presented both the server certificate, ***.openvpn.net**, as well as the intermediate CA certificate, **Go Daddy Secure Certificate Authority – G2**:

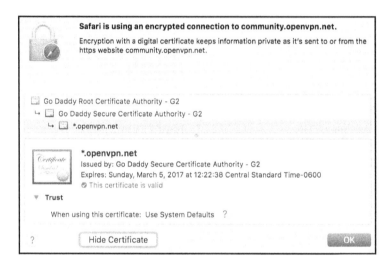

In nearly every OpenVPN configuration I have seen deployed, the CA is going to be a self-signed unit that will not pre-exist in the operating system trust store. Some larger corporations might have a large PKI deployed, so may have several CAs deployed on client workstations, but this is likely an exception to the rule.

For this reason, OpenVPN client packages will contain, at a minimum, a configuration file and the CA certificate. These can be combined using inline certificates, which embed the CA certificate data within the configuration file. If this data is not embedded, it will need to be bundled as a separate file. Most clients will require many pieces of certificate data: the CA certificate, the client certificate, and the client key. All of these can be embedded inline:

```
● ● ●                        author@client

author@client:~-> cat config.ovpn
dev tun
client
proto udp
port 1194
remote 192.168.19.37

<ca>
-----BEGIN CERTIFICATE-----
MIID+zCCA2SgAwIBAgIJAMknjCzAGI0OMA0GCSqGSIb3DQEBBAUAMIGlMQswCQYD
VQQGEwJVUzESMBAGA1UECBMJTWlubmVzb3RhMRAwDgYDVQQHEwdTdCBQYXVsMSEw
HwYDVQQKExhUcm91YmxlIFNob290aW5nIE9wZW5WUE4xITAfBgNVBAMTGFRyb3Vi
bGUgU2hvb3RpbmcgT3BlblZQTjEqMCgGCSqGSIb3DQEJARYbZWNyYXN0N0QHNlY3Vy
ZS1jb21wdXRpbmcubmV0MB4XDTE2MDgwMTE2MjgzMFoXDTI2MDczMDE2MjgzMFow
gaUxCzAJBgNVBAYTAlVTMRIwEAYDVQQIEwlNaW5uZXNvdGExEDAOBgNVBAcTB1N0
IFBhdWwxITAfBgNVBAoTGFRyb3VibGUgU2hvb3RpbmcgT3BlblZQTjEhMB8GA1UE
AxMYVHJvdWJsZSBTaG9vdGluZyBPcGVuVlBOMSowKAYJKoZIhvcNAQkBFhtlY3Jp
c3RAc2VjdXJlLWNvbXB1dGluZy5uZXQwgZ8wDQYJKoZIhvcNAQEBBQADgY0AMIGJ
AoGBALb01zWfDC74aX+gdOgh1/xeOJGPSKTAiy5xHg5GdXjDppEYu/Arg2SpoDka
hxMH4PzOJsxxNq4NUBFU+ulQze1sAwUO8eEBnQbGTL90u8woBbvi0bLRDK9hEea1
jkFLH4iF22gHMS5obTZNEe4Ks0DMB8+2M5fK+kxuZsmPcTjZAgMBAAGjggEvMIIB
KzAMBgNVHRMEBTADAQH/MB0GA1UdDgQWBBT7Vjj7PrjNmsHutKvlLDQDD+c6lzCB
2gYDVR0jBIHSMIHPgBT7Vjj7PrjNmsHutKvlLDQDD+c6l6GBq6SBqDCBpTELMAkG
A1UEBhMCVVMxEjAQBgNVBAgTCU1pbm5lc290YTEQMA4GA1UEBxMHU3QgUGF1bDEh
MB8GA1UEChMYVHJvdWJsZSBTaG9vdGluZyBPcGVuVlBOMSEwHwYDVQQDExhUcm91
YmxlIFNob290aW5nIE9wZW5WUE4xKjAoBgkqhkiG9w0BCQEWG2VjcmlzdEBzZWN1
cmUtY29tcHV0aW5nLm5ldIIJAMknjCzAGI0OMB8GA1UdHwQYMBYwFKASoBCGDmh0
dHA6Ly9DUkxxfVVJJMA0GCSqGSIb3DQEBBAUAA4GBAIiJI2MNAsyKasz/187Rc6rm
tkHcK7BHK2tMb7evlu5xcl4XYdwHo5HsK8Vfccn9FhZX/NokzVq3v+ModStpcXDr
4jiE88xXMj2uRU+cJMBy0WpujuzwY+GWOe8r70HBn+AizodBN8QbqfQfQbmNxVT1
zRFDuFhr/14PUxbhbHy4
-----END CERTIFICATE-----
```

Embedded CA certificate payload within OpenVPN client configuration file (some content truncated at the bottom)

Regardless of how you develop your certificate chain, it is important that the clients and server be given all the necessary certificates to establish a full chain of trust. Missing components within the chain will result in validation and verification errors, preventing successful connections. It is not enough to include only the topmost root CA certificate; intermediate/sub CAs must also be included.

Using the OpenVPN community server certificate, we can leverage the OpenSSL `verify` command to verify a certificate chain. This is pretty simple with a single root certificate and a single client certificate, but gets more complicated when an intermediate CA is involved.

I downloaded the certificate chain via the *SSL Labs* interface, but there are many ways to download the chain. The certificate details will be available from the Packt website at `https://www.packtpub.com/networking-and-servers/troubleshooting-openvpn`. I ended up with three files after separating the details.

It required two commands to fully verify this chain. First, OpenSSL expects the certificate that is passed with CA file to be a self-signed CA certificate (all root CAs are actually self-signed). It will not recognize the intermediate certificate as a CA file, since it is not self-signed, but signed by the root CA.

For the first step, I verified the intermediate certificate against the CA. The second step listed the intermediate using the -untrusted option followed by the final server certificate. In the following output, you can see the list of files and the result of the verification commands:

```
author@client:~/covpn.verify-> ls -larth
total 16
-rw-rw-r--    1 ecrist  staff   1.3K Nov 25 10:14 ca-root.crt
-rw-rw-r--    1 ecrist  staff   1.7K Nov 25 10:15 ca-int.crt
-rw-rw-r--    1 ecrist  staff   1.8K Nov 25 10:15 server.crt
drwxr-xr-x+ 376 ecrist  staff    12K Nov 25 10:15 ..
drwxrwxr-x    6 ecrist  staff   204B Nov 25 10:26 .
-rw-rw-r--    1 ecrist  staff   3.0K Nov 25 10:27 ca.crt
author@client:~/covpn.verify-> openssl verify -CAfile ca-root.crt ca-int.crt
ca-int.crt: OK
author@client:~/covpn.verify-> openssl verify -CAfile ca-root.crt -untrusted ca-int.crt server.crt
server.crt: OK
author@client:~/covpn.verify->
```

OpenSSL certificate chain verification

The Certificate Revocation List

Thus far, we have only talked about trusting certificates and the overall chain of that trust. Another important component and feature of the X.509 standard is the **Certificate Revocation List** (**CRL**). The purpose of the CRL is to provide affirmative information to interested systems about which certificates should no longer be trusted. Querying the CRL or refusing to trust certificates contained within the CRL is ultimately determined by the client.

There are many reasons to revoke a particular certificate. For global PKI systems, a server certificate key may have been exposed or lost, or the operator may have needed to change the **common name** (**CN**) of the certificate.

In the case of OpenVPN, a user certificate may be added to the local CRL because the employee left the company, or perhaps a given OpenVPN server has been decommissioned so that server certificate is no longer required.

It is best practice to deploy the CRL with OpenVPN on the server side. Technically speaking, it is possible to deploy the CRL on the client side, as well, but the utility is limited and the logistics of pushing an updated CRL to clients is difficult. There is talk of OpenVPN 3.0 adding support for **CRL Distribution Points** (**CDPs**) that would allow the client to query a special URL, LDAP, or other source to pull *on-the-fly* CRL data.

When the OpenVPN server is deployed with CRL, it will be queried every time a client connects or the certificate handshake reoccurs. The following screenshots show the client side of a connection that was initiated with a revoked client certificate. As of OpenVPN 2.3.13, there is no message passed to the client indicating a connection failure is due to a revoked certificate. Instead, the connection dies with an interrupted system call message:

```
● ● ●                                    author@client
Fri Nov 25 09:52:41 2016 us=707312   port_share_host = '[UNDEF]'
Fri Nov 25 09:52:41 2016 us=707315   port_share_port = 0
Fri Nov 25 09:52:41 2016 us=707319   client = ENABLED
Fri Nov 25 09:52:41 2016 us=707323   pull = ENABLED
Fri Nov 25 09:52:41 2016 us=707327   auth_user_pass_file = '[UNDEF]'
Fri Nov 25 09:52:41 2016 us=707332 OpenVPN 2.3.13 x86_64-apple-darwin [SSL (OpenSSL)] [LZO] [PKCS11] [MH] [IPv6] built on N
ov 17 2016
Fri Nov 25 09:52:41 2016 us=707340 library versions: OpenSSL 1.0.2j  26 Sep 2016, LZO 2.09
Fri Nov 25 09:52:41 2016 us=707430 WARNING: No server certificate verification method has been enabled.  See http://openvpn
.net/howto.html#mitm for more info.
Fri Nov 25 09:52:41 2016 us=708068 Control Channel MTU parms [ L:1541 D:1212 EF:38 EB:0 ET:0 EL:3 ]
Fri Nov 25 09:52:41 2016 us=708128 Socket Buffers: R=[196724->196724] S=[9216->9216]
Fri Nov 25 09:52:41 2016 us=708832 Data Channel MTU parms [ L:1541 D:1450 EF:41 EB:12 ET:0 EL:3 ]
Fri Nov 25 09:52:41 2016 us=708854 Local Options String: 'V4,dev-type tun,link-mtu 1541,tun-mtu 1500,proto UDPv4,cipher BF-
CBC,auth SHA1,keysize 128,key-method 2,tls-client'
Fri Nov 25 09:52:41 2016 us=708860 Expected Remote Options String: 'V4,dev-type tun,link-mtu 1541,tun-mtu 1500,proto UDPv4,
cipher BF-CBC,auth SHA1,keysize 128,key-method 2,tls-server'
Fri Nov 25 09:52:41 2016 us=708870 Local Options hash (VER=V4): '3514370b'
Fri Nov 25 09:52:41 2016 us=708876 Expected Remote Options hash (VER=V4): '239669a8'
Fri Nov 25 09:52:41 2016 us=708889 UDPv4 link local (bound): [undef]
Fri Nov 25 09:52:41 2016 us=708895 UDPv4 link remote: [AF_INET]192.168.19.37:1194
Fri Nov 25 09:52:41 2016 us=712626 TLS: Initial packet from [AF_INET]192.168.19.37:1194, sid=84128882 1a31f3e4
Fri Nov 25 09:52:41 2016 us=746857 VERIFY OK: depth=1, C=US, ST=Minnesota, L=St Paul, O=Trouble Shooting OpenVPN, CN=Troubl
e Shooting OpenVPN, emailAddress=ecrist@secure-computing.net
Fri Nov 25 09:52:41 2016 us=747571 VERIFY OK: depth=0, C=US, ST=Minnesota, O=Trouble Shooting OpenVPN, CN=tshoot-server, em
ailAddress=ecrist@secure-computing.net
^CFri Nov 25 09:52:43 2016 us=677308 event_wait : Interrupted system call (code=4)
Fri Nov 25 09:52:43 2016 us=677602 TCP/UDP: Closing socket
Fri Nov 25 09:52:43 2016 us=677729 SIGINT[hard,] received, process exiting
author@client:~>
```

Client side: connected with revoked certificate – no CRL error listed

On the server side, however, we are given a very clear CRL error (highlighted content):

```
● ● ●                                    author@server
Fri Nov 25 02:44:22 2016 us=243312 MULTI: multi_create_instance called
Fri Nov 25 02:44:22 2016 us=243343 192.168.19.104:1194 Re-using SSL/TLS context
Fri Nov 25 02:44:22 2016 us=243432 192.168.19.104:1194 Control Channel MTU parms [ L:1541 D:1212 EF:38 EB:0 ET:0 EL:3 ]
Fri Nov 25 02:44:22 2016 us=243440 192.168.19.104:1194 Data Channel MTU parms [ L:1541 D:1450 EF:41 EB:12 ET:0 EL:3 ]
Fri Nov 25 02:44:22 2016 us=243464 192.168.19.104:1194 Local Options String: 'V4,dev-type tun,link-mtu 1541,tun-mtu 1500,pr
oto UDPv4,cipher BF-CBC,auth SHA1,keysize 128,key-method 2,tls-server'
Fri Nov 25 02:44:22 2016 us=243469 192.168.19.104:1194 Expected Remote Options String: 'V4,dev-type tun,link-mtu 1541,tun-m
tu 1500,proto UDPv4,cipher BF-CBC,auth SHA1,keysize 128,key-method 2,tls-client'
Fri Nov 25 02:44:22 2016 us=243486 192.168.19.104:1194 Local Options hash (VER=V4): '239669a8'
Fri Nov 25 02:44:22 2016 us=243495 192.168.19.104:1194 Expected Remote Options hash (VER=V4): '3514370b'
Fri Nov 25 02:44:22 2016 us=243515 192.168.19.104:1194 TLS: Initial packet from [AF_INET]192.168.19.104:1194, sid=e9407daf
7da54daa
Fri Nov 25 02:44:22 2016 us=297211 192.168.19.104:1194 CRL CHECK OK: C=US, ST=Minnesota, L=St Paul, O=Trouble Shooting Open
VPN, CN=Trouble Shooting OpenVPN, emailAddress=ecrist@secure-computing.net
Fri Nov 25 02:44:22 2016 us=297234 192.168.19.104:1194 VERIFY OK: depth=1, C=US, ST=Minnesota, L=St Paul, O=Trouble Shootin
g OpenVPN, CN=Trouble Shooting OpenVPN, emailAddress=ecrist@secure-computing.net
Fri Nov 25 02:44:22 2016 us=297347 192.168.19.104:1194 CRL CHECK FAILED: C=US, ST=Minnesota, O=Trouble Shooting OpenVPN, CN
=tshoot-revoke, emailAddress=ecrist@secure-computing.net (serial 03) is REVOKED
Fri Nov 25 02:44:22 2016 us=297397 192.168.19.104:1194 OpenSSL: error:140890B2:SSL routines:SSL3_GET_CLIENT_CERTIFICATE:no
certificate returned
Fri Nov 25 02:44:22 2016 us=297404 192.168.19.104:1194 TLS_ERROR: BIO read tls_read_plaintext error
Fri Nov 25 02:44:22 2016 us=297410 192.168.19.104:1194 TLS Error: TLS object -> incoming plaintext read error
Fri Nov 25 02:44:22 2016 us=297413 192.168.19.104:1194 TLS Error: TLS handshake failed
Fri Nov 25 02:44:22 2016 us=297465 192.168.19.104:1194 SIGUSR1[soft,tls-error] received, client-instance restarting
^CFri Nov 25 02:44:32 2016 us=313525 event_wait : Interrupted system call (code=4)
Fri Nov 25 02:44:32 2016 us=313652 TCP/UDP: Closing socket
Fri Nov 25 02:44:32 2016 us=313677 Closing TUN/TAP interface
Fri Nov 25 02:44:32 2016 us=313829 /sbin/ifconfig tun0 destroy
Fri Nov 25 02:44:32 2016 us=314997 SIGINT[hard,] received, process exiting
author@server:/usr/local/etc/openvpn-> ▐
```

Server side: client CRL error with revoked certificate

In the preceding message, OpenVPN indicates that a CRL check failed and calls out the serial number of the certificate. We can verify this by querying the CRL file directly using the OpenSSL command-line utility with the following command:

```
author@server:/usr/local/etc/openvpn-> openssl crl
-noout -text -in ../ssl-admin/prog/crl.pem
```

The command option earlier puts OpenSSL in the CRL mode, does not output a file, outputs the CRL in text form, and reads in the CRL file from `../ssl-admin/prog/crl.pem`. Finally, in the output, we can see the presence of serial number (`03`), the timestamp of the revocation, and the signature of the certificate:

Inspecting the CRL and identifying serial number 03

System date and time

An important piece of data within an X.509 certificate is the timestamp indicated when a certificate becomes valid and when it expires. Outside the time frame specified with the certificate, it is to be untrusted or invalid. If the time is incorrect on a client system, the OpenVPN server, or the system that generated the signed certificates, then the certificate validity could be negatively impacted.

The following screenshot shows the OpenVPN community website's SSL certificate. The highlighted section illustrates the start and stop of validity with **Not Valid Before** and **Not Valid After**. In the case of this example, the certificate begins validity on **Monday, February 29, 2016 at 12:06:39 Central Standard Time-0600**.

This certificate is considered invalid after **Sunday, March 5, 2017 at 12:22:38 Central Standard Time-0600**:

Since I took this screenshot within this time frame (Wednesday, November 16, 2016 at 05:32:23 CST), the certificate shows as valid. If I change the time on my laptop by jumping a year ahead, the validity changes. In this case, my laptop considered the date and time to be Thursday, November 16, 2017 at 05:41:44 and the certificate is marked as expired:

Similarly, if we set the date on the local machine to a date and time prior to when the certificate is valid, we get a message indicating that it is not yet valid:

It is recommended that all systems participating in PKI utilize **Network Time Protocol (NTP)** or some other trusted mechanism to keep the system time current and in sync. **National Institute of Standards and Technology (NIST)** maintains a list of publicly accessible NTP servers. You can view their list by navigating to `http://tf.nist.gov/tf-cgi/servers.cgi`. The NTP Pool Project also maintains a large pool of publicly available NTP servers around the world. More information and server addresses are available at `http://www.pool.ntp.org/en/`.

It is just as important for the system signing and issuing certificates to have the correct time as it is for the client.

Further details of the X.509 standard, including PKI, certificates, and CRLs can be found in the two IETF documents: RFC 2459 (`https://tools.ietf.org/html/rfc2459`) and RFC 5280 (`https://tools.ietf.org/html/rfc5280`).

Authentication and plugins

Apart from X.509 tools, OpenVPN provides a mechanism to use authentication plugins along with client connection scripts. It is possible to remove the requirement for client certificates using `--client-cert-not-required` (deprecated in 2.4, removed in 2.5 in favor of `--verify-client-cert`). In this case, authentication rests solely upon the `--auth-user-pass-verify` option.

If `--client-config-dir` is still desired without client certificates, you will need to leverage `--username-as-common-name`. Of course, if you're going to require usernames and passwords, it is necessary to add the `--auth-user-pass` option to all the client configuration files.

The `--auth-user-pass-verify` script is the last in a long chain of scripts that are run. The majority of environment details are available to all of these scripts, including the CN. If you are troubleshooting problems with this script, ensure that the connection is not being killed due to logic in other script routines prior to reaching your authentication script.

Usernames and passwords

OpenVPN can read usernames and passwords from a file, preventing a prompt on the client side. Early versions of the OpenVPN GUI were compiled with this option disabled. The compile was changed with the first 2.2 release candidate in February of 2011. This is used with the `--auth-user-pass <file>` option where `<file>` is the path to a file containing the username and password on separate lines.

--ccd-exclusive

The `--client-config-dir` option is often used to apply client-specific configuration and routing. OpenVPN provides a related option, `--ccd-exclusive`, which will prevent client connections from clients who do not have a file in the `client-config` directory. When this option is present, even an empty file named to match the CN is sufficient to meet this constraint.

Unlike some of the certificate errors, failing this check does at least provide an authentication error to the client, though it is somewhat generic:

```
●  ◉  ●                              author@client

author@client:~-> /Applications/Tunnelblick.app/Contents/Resources/openvpn/openvpn-2.3.13-openssl-1.0.2j/openvpn config.ovp
n
Fri Nov 25 11:11:36 2016 OpenVPN 2.3.13 x86_64-apple-darwin [SSL (OpenSSL)] [LZO] [PKCS11] [MH] [IPv6] built on Nov 17 2016
Fri Nov 25 11:11:36 2016 library versions: OpenSSL 1.0.2j  26 Sep 2016, LZO 2.09
Fri Nov 25 11:11:36 2016 WARNING: No server certificate verification method has been enabled.  See http://openvpn.net/howto
.html#mitm for more info.
Fri Nov 25 11:11:36 2016 UDPv4 link local (bound): [undef]
Fri Nov 25 11:11:36 2016 UDPv4 link remote: [AF_INET]192.168.19.37:1194
Fri Nov 25 11:11:36 2016 WARNING: INSECURE cipher with block size less than 128 bit (64 bit).  This allows attacks like SWE
ET32.  Mitigate by using a --cipher with a larger block size (e.g. AES-256-CBC).
Fri Nov 25 11:11:36 2016 WARNING: INSECURE cipher with block size less than 128 bit (64 bit).  This allows attacks like SWE
ET32.  Mitigate by using a --cipher with a larger block size (e.g. AES-256-CBC).
Fri Nov 25 11:11:36 2016 [tshoot-server] Peer Connection Initiated with [AF_INET]192.168.19.37:1194
Fri Nov 25 11:11:38 2016 AUTH: Received control message: AUTH_FAILED
Fri Nov 25 11:11:38 2016 SIGTERM[soft,auth-failure] received, process exiting
author@client:~->
```

Client side: AUTH_FAILED is apparent in the log file

The server-side log, however, does contain the reason for the authentication error (highlighted). Also, further down, you can see the `push` command for the AUTH_FAILED message to the client:

```
●  ●  ●                           author@server
Fri Nov 25 04:03:16 2016 us=653767 192.168.19.104:1194 Re-using SSL/TLS context
Fri Nov 25 04:03:16 2016 us=653856 192.168.19.104:1194 Control Channel MTU parms [ L:1541 D:1212 EF:38 EB:0 ET:0 EL:3 ]
Fri Nov 25 04:03:16 2016 us=653865 192.168.19.104:1194 Data Channel MTU parms [ L:1541 D:1450 EF:41 EB:12 ET:0 EL:3 ]
Fri Nov 25 04:03:16 2016 us=653889 192.168.19.104:1194 Local Options String: 'V4,dev-type tun,link-mtu 1541,tun-mtu 1500,pr
oto UDPv4,cipher BF-CBC,auth SHA1,keysize 128,key-method 2,tls-server'
Fri Nov 25 04:03:16 2016 us=653894 192.168.19.104:1194 Expected Remote Options String: 'V4,dev-type tun,link-mtu 1541,tun-m
tu 1500,proto UDPv4,cipher BF-CBC,auth SHA1,keysize 128,key-method 2,tls-client'
Fri Nov 25 04:03:16 2016 us=653911 192.168.19.104:1194 Local Options hash (VER=V4): '239669a8'
Fri Nov 25 04:03:16 2016 us=653920 192.168.19.104:1194 Expected Remote Options hash (VER=V4): '3514370b'
Fri Nov 25 04:03:16 2016 us=653941 192.168.19.104:1194 TLS: Initial packet from [AF_INET]192.168.19.104:1194, sid=478ab1f6
07eb559b
Fri Nov 25 04:03:16 2016 us=664351 192.168.19.104:1194 CRL CHECK OK: C=US, ST=Minnesota, L=St Paul, O=Trouble Shooting Open
VPN, CN=Trouble Shooting OpenVPN, emailAddress=ecrist@secure-computing.net
Fri Nov 25 04:03:16 2016 us=664375 192.168.19.104:1194 VERIFY OK: depth=1, C=US, ST=Minnesota, L=St Paul, O=Trouble Shootin
g OpenVPN, CN=Trouble Shooting OpenVPN, emailAddress=ecrist@secure-computing.net
Fri Nov 25 04:03:16 2016 us=664491 192.168.19.104:1194 CRL CHECK OK: C=US, ST=Minnesota, O=Trouble Shooting OpenVPN, CN=tsh
oot-client, emailAddress=ecrist@secure-computing.net
Fri Nov 25 04:03:16 2016 us=664505 192.168.19.104:1194 VERIFY OK: depth=0, C=US, ST=Minnesota, O=Trouble Shooting OpenVPN,
CN=tshoot-client, emailAddress=ecrist@secure-computing.net
Fri Nov 25 04:03:16 2016 us=666571 192.168.19.104:1194 TLS Auth Error: --client-config-dir authentication failed for common
 name 'tshoot-client' file='ccd/tshoot-client'
Fri Nov 25 04:03:16 2016 us=669738 192.168.19.104:1194 Control Channel: TLSv1.2, cipher TLSv1/SSLv3 DHE-RSA-AES256-GCM-SHA3
84, 1024 bit RSA
Fri Nov 25 04:03:16 2016 us=669752 192.168.19.104:1194 [tshoot-client] Peer Connection Initiated with [AF_INET]192.168.19.1
04:1194
Fri Nov 25 04:03:18 2016 us=709105 192.168.19.104:1194 PUSH: Received control message: 'PUSH_REQUEST'
Fri Nov 25 04:03:18 2016 us=709122 192.168.19.104:1194 Delayed exit in 5 seconds
Fri Nov 25 04:03:18 2016 us=709130 192.168.19.104:1194 SENT CONTROL [tshoot-client]: 'AUTH_FAILED' (status=1)
Fri Nov 25 04:03:24 2016 us=112198 192.168.19.104:1194 SIGTERM[soft,delayed-exit] received, client-instance exiting
```

Server side: authentication error with cause identified

Summary

This chapter has helped to illustrate some of the inner workings of the X.509 standard. My goal was to demystify certificate chains and the revocation list by providing tools and real-world command examples and allowing an OpenVPN administrator to identify connection and authentication problems.

Due to some limitations of how OpenVPN implemented these standards, useful clues are not always present in the client-side logs. Some of the most common and difficult-to-diagnose problems have been identified with solutions or explanation of how the logic is executed within the OpenVPN binary.

7
Network and Routing

Building a network is the core functionality OpenVPN provides. The complexity of the network is up to the administrator, but I have seen this range from a simple client/server with a few resources on a local network to VPN chaining, client-side routing, and the encapsulation of other network streams.

In order to build a quality virtual private network, it is necessary to understand how to troubleshoot issues. In addition, it is useful to understand how some of these network topologies relate to OpenVPN. This chapter will help with all of these concepts.

Connectivity

The first step in connecting to a remote VPN server is actually having the ability to connect outbound from the current network, whether that is from home, a coffee shop, a corporate network, or via your favorite mobile hotspot. If the outbound connection is blocked, none of the other configurations will matter.

Inbound connection–server

On the server side, connectivity can prove a bit more difficult. The OpenVPN server needs to either reside directly on the public network, or port-forwarding rules need to be applied to deliver the traffic to the correct system. All servers used across the general Internet will require some form of routable or public IP address.

I will cover both a simple public address case in addition to the slightly more complicated port-redirection case. It is good to keep in mind that many corporate networks will seldom place the VPN server directly on the public Internet. Instead, they will usually use multiple layers of firewalls, **intrusion detection system** (**IDS**), and **intrusion prevention system** (**IPS**). The following illustration demonstrates one of these more complicated scenarios:

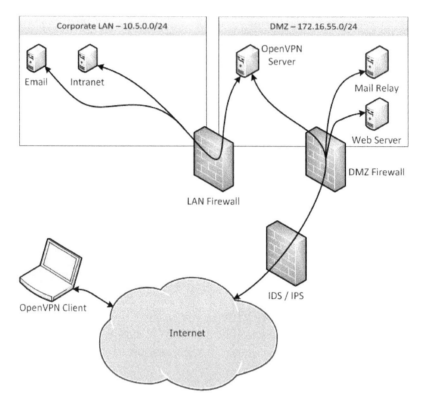

Corporate deployment using DMZ and multiple firewalls and IDS/IPS

The arrows in the preceding image demonstrate the path traffic would take from a potential client system. Note that both *public* traffic (that is, traffic destined for hosts available on the general Internet) and the VPN traffic to internal systems traverse the IDS/IPS system(s) and the DMZ firewall. Then, the OpenVPN traffic must traverse the server and the LAN firewall before finally reaching the internal systems.

The method most commonly used for addressing these systems involves multiple routes and some **network address translation** (**NAT**). The systems within a **demilitarized zone** (**DMZ**) will normally have a real public IP associated with them, generally hosted on either the firewall or IDS/IPS system, often known as a **virtual IP** (**VIP**).

VIPs will be publicly routable addresses. The hosting system will forward traffic, after inspection and rule checks, to the internal system within the DMZ. Traffic will then flow from the DMZ-hosted system to the next destination. In the case of our OpenVPN server, it will forward that traffic into LAN after some final firewall policy checks by the LAN firewall.

This configuration is much more secure than most typical OpenVPN setups where the server resides directly on the Internet. These configurations, however, are complex, and can be much more complicated than the server administrator requires or even understands.

Publicly addressed server

Having the ability to assign a public IP address directly on your OpenVPN is the easiest method of hosting a server. Hosting an OpenVPN server at a VPS provider is likely the simplest deployment method. Advantages of this include commercial-quality uplinks, server and hardware reliability, and you can run these virtual servers at a multitude of providers in geographically convenient locations. This allows the administrator to place the VPN server closer to the users of that system and lowers latency and potential bandwidth bottlenecks:

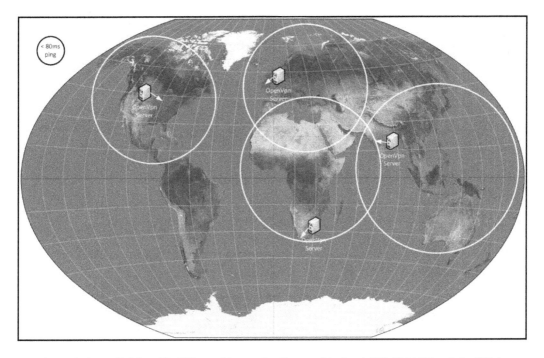

An example of geographically located OpenVPN servers (Map source: https://commons.wikimedia.org/wiki/File:Winkel_triple_projection_SW.jpg)

Multiple OpenVPN `--remote` options can be specified in client configuration files, and they will be tried in the order listed. Some OpenVPN service providers allow users to generate their configuration file based on their geographical location, resulting in a series of `--remote` entries optimized for that user's location.

Fortunately for the novice or aspiring VPN administrator, the majority of VPS providers place the system directly on the public Internet. Depending on the operating system and VPS provider, some systems may come preconfigured with some basic firewall rules. Tweaking and verifying these is covered in a later section.

There are a couple of things you can do, however, to ensure the OpenVPN process is listening for new connections. Both Unix and Windows systems use the `netstat` command to list open ports. This command, depending on the arguments, will display both outbound connections as well as ports opened by listening services. On Unix, you can use the `grep` command to filter the results, looking for the listening port. On Windows, you can filter with the `findstr` filter.

The following screenshots show what this would look like for both a Windows and a FreeBSD server. Linux or other *nix flavors will behave similarly:

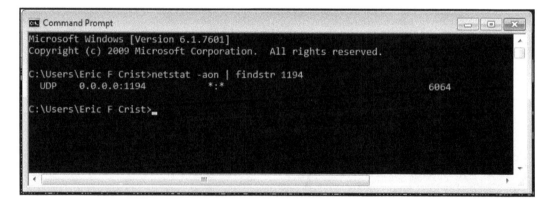

Identifying the listening OpenVPN process on Windows

The `-aon` command-line options specify to list all sockets, numerically, and by process ID. If you have administrative privileges, you can add the `-b` option, which will identify the process name:

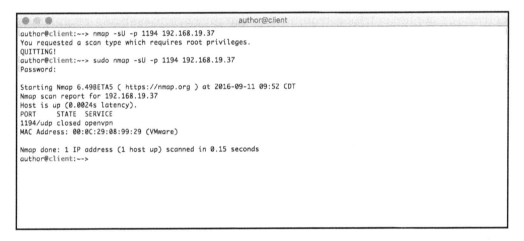

```
                              ecrist@meow
root@tshoot-srvr:~ # netstat -an | grep 1194
udp4       0       0 *.1194                     *.*
root@tshoot-srvr:~ #
```

Showing the listening port for OpenVPN on FreeBSD

You can use the `netcat` or `nmap` utilities to verify that the port is open from a remote system. A remote verification helps to ensure that all the necessary firewall rules are in place to allow the traffic:

```
                              author@client
author@client:~-> nmap -sU -p 1194 192.168.19.37
You requested a scan type which requires root privileges.
QUITTING!
author@client:~-> sudo nmap -sU -p 1194 192.168.19.37
Password:

Starting Nmap 6.49BETA5 ( https://nmap.org ) at 2016-09-11 09:52 CDT
Nmap scan report for 192.168.19.37
Host is up (0.0024s latency).
PORT      STATE  SERVICE
1194/udp closed openvpn
MAC Address: 00:0C:29:08:99:29 (VMware)

Nmap done: 1 IP address (1 host up) scanned in 0.15 seconds
author@client:~->
```

nmap output testing UDP port 1194 on OS X

On *nix operating systems, the `nmap` command requires root privileges to scan UDP ports. The UDP protocol is a best-effort dispatch meaning that the sender will not wait for a confirmation before sending the next packet. TCP, on the other hand, will respond with packet reception data and request retransmission of lost or corrupt packets.

Because of this behavior, `nmap` requires extra privileges to intercept ICMP messages from the kernel as UDP does not provide the data needed alone:

```
                                                        author@client
author@client:~-> nc -vz -u 192.168.19.37 1194
found 0 associations
found 1 connections:
     1: flags=82<CONNECTED,PREFERRED>
        outif (null)
        src 192.168.19.104 port 53604
        dst 192.168.19.37 port 1194
        rank info not available

Connection to 192.168.19.37 port 1194 [udp/openvpn] succeeded!
author@client:~-> ▒
```

netcat does not require root and serves the necessary role

The `ncat` (or `netcat` or `nc`) command does not require root permissions. On Windows, neither the `nmap` nor `netcat` tools require administrative permissions. As a regular user, I was able to run both without escalated privileges. The Windows tools provide a nice graphical interface, but the overall end result and command syntax proves identical to the *nix version of the tool.

The command shown in the following screenshot is identical to what you would run on the Linux command line:

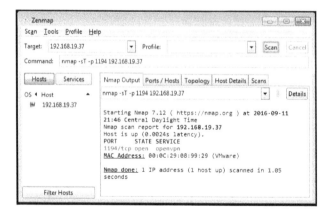

Both tools are available across both the *nix and Windows platforms though are seldom part of the base distribution. You can download them both by going to `http://nmap.org/download.html` for `netcat` and `nmap`. The single Windows setup will, by default, install both utilities, along with some other useful ones not covered here.

Privately addressed server with port forwarding

Hosting an OpenVPN server on a home network connection provides its own benefits and complications. This is most often deployed when someone wants to access resources at home remotely. Some examples include network file servers hosting photos and movies or a home printer or a DVR.

The primary complication with hosting on a typical home or consumer Internet connection is the single IP address, which is most often not a static address. In this case, the **customer premises equipment** (**CPE**) will hold the public IP address. Often, CPE is an ISP-provided piece of equipment that offers a limited subset of configuration options and capabilities. This could also be an off-the-shelf system such as an Apple AirPort, an OpenWrt device, or any other home router.

Common functionality should include some firewalling capabilities along with some rudimentary port forwarding. High-end units will allow the configuration of **Dynamic DNS** (**DynDNS**) registration. For the purposes of this example, we will only focus on port forwarding. In addition, we will assume a static IP address. The majority of providers charge extra for a truly static IP address, but it is common according to Internet testimonials to retain the same public IP for a single CPE for many months or even beyond a year.

With port forwarding, an administrator will take a port on a publicly accessible system, in our case our CPE, and forward that connection to an internal system. The default port for SSH, for example, is 22. If we wanted to host an SSH server on a couple of internal systems, we could forward port 22 from our CPE to internal system 1. The second system, however, would have to be a separate port (any arbitrary port) since 22 is now used.

In the earlier-mentioned scenario, let us assume the public IP address is `192.0.2.5`. Our internal network is using `172.31.0.0/24`, with our two SSH servers at `172.31.0.9` and `172.31.0.43`. We can redirect port `22` from our CPE to server 1 (x.9), but we need to use another port, `774` (or any arbitrary port), with our second server (x.43):

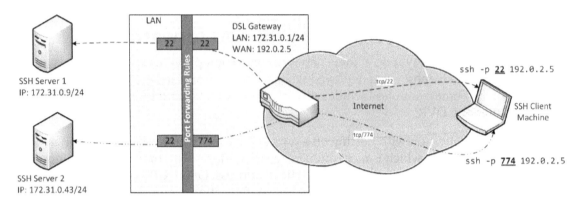

A relationship of internal hosts to CPE in port-forwarding setup

Our SSH session initiation would look as follows:

> **author@client:~-> ssh -p 22 user@192.0.2.5 user@172.31.0.9:~->author@client:~-> ssh -p 774 user@192.0.2.5 user@172.31.0.43:~->**

Note that, in both cases, the external IP is identical, but the port number changes. Also, the internal host we connect to changes, but the SSH process on each host remains on the default *tcp/22*. I will touch on it further in the firewall section later in this chapter, but it is important that those internal hosts have outbound access to hosts connecting in order to establish those connections.

For testing our port-forwarding rule for *udp/1194* on a typical home network, we are forwarding *udp/1194* on our public interface on a Ubiquiti EdgeMAX router to our internal OpenVPN server on `192.168.19.37`:

Ubiquiti EdgeMAX port-forwarding configuration

The configuration on this device takes a few details, including the following:

- Internal IP address: 192.168.19.37
- Internal port: 1194
- **Protocol**: **UDP**
- External IP address: Your actual public IP (the test here used a real port forward over the Internet; our public IP is blurred)
- External port: 1194 (this does not need to match; internal and external can be whatever you choose)

For the inbound interface, I selected **pppoe0** since this is the interface that holds the publicly routable IP address. Once the configuration is saved, it is live and ready to be used.

To test the new rule, we will use the `netcat` utility, without starting up the OpenVPN process. This allows for a simple test where we are sending raw text across the port. On the server, shut down the OpenVPN process if it is running, and execute the following command:

```
author@server:-~> nc -ukl 1194
```

This command opens *udp/1194* and listens for incoming connections. The `-k` option keeps `netcat` listening for additional connections. Because we are using UDP, there is no real concept of a stateful connection, so every packet is a new connection.

Next, from outside the network, again using `netcat`, make an outgoing connection to the public IP and port combination used for your port-forwarding rule. On the external test system, run the following command:

```
author@external:-~> nc -u 203.0.113.9 1194
```

With both windows open, you should be able to type into the external window and see the message appear on the OpenVPN server console after each press of the enter key. If you do not see your messages on the server console, there is either a problem with your port-forwarding rule, or there may be a firewall somewhere in the path that is blocking the traffic.

Here is our console session on the internal OpenVPN server after our successful test, as described earlier. The communication for this test is only one-way, so typing a message on the server console will not send a message back to the test client:

```
author@server:~-> nc -ukl 1194
Is this thing on?
Typing from the remote client.
Typing from the server console.
Typing again from the remote client.  No server message seen.
```

Internal OpenVPN server with test UDP listening running

The following screenshot shows the messages sent by simply typing into the window and pressing *Enter*. All the messages show up on the server, but note the message typed on the server did not show up in the client window; this is normal:

```
● ◉ ●                        ecrist@terrance
ecrist@terrance:~-> nc -u    203.0.113.9    1194
Is this thing on?
Typing from the remote client.
Typing again from the remote client.  No server message seen.
```

External test system with open connection to public IP on udp/1194

Outbound connection–client

Much of the testing demonstrated in the previous section properly illustrates testing outgoing connections during the testing of the incoming connections. It should be readily apparent that if an outgoing connection fails, the incoming connection on the other end would not succeed.

It needs to be pointed out that testing for open UDP ports can be problematic. The netcat tool, for example, gives frequent false positives, depending on the remote operating system and firewall policies.

In all of our examples, we have used *udp/1194*, which is the OpenVPN IANA-assigned port. If we use netcat to test *udp/1000*, for which we do not have a listening daemon, the remote FreeBSD system, combined with the netcat tool's internal logic, lists the port as open.

If we use `nmap`, however, we can see that the port is correctly identified as closed:

```
author@client
author@client:~-> nc -vz -u 192.168.19.37 1000
found 0 associations
found 1 connections:
     1: flags=82<CONNECTED,PREFERRED>
        outif (null)
        src 192.168.19.104 port 55598
        dst 192.168.19.37 port 1000
        rank info not available

Connection to 192.168.19.37 port 1000 [udp/cadlock2] succeeded!
author@client:~-> sudo nmap -sU -p 1000 192.168.19.37
Password:

Starting Nmap 6.49BETA5 ( https://nmap.org ) at 2016-09-12 21:16 CDT
Nmap scan report for 192.168.19.37
Host is up (0.0016s latency).
PORT     STATE  SERVICE
1000/udp closed ock
MAC Address: 00:0C:29:08:99:29 (VMware)

Nmap done: 1 IP address (1 host up) scanned in 0.15 seconds
author@client:~-> ▊
```

Demonstrating differing results between nmap and netcat for a closed port

Digital Internals has a decent write-up discussing the false positives at
`http://www.digitalinternals.com/unix/unix-linux-netcat-check-port-open/511/`.

Firewall filters and inspection

Some service providers block the *default port 1194* (both TCP and UDP) from some client networks. Corporate networks, as an easy example, block most inbound traffic to the network, preventing a rogue service like a web server or OpenVPN server. On a much larger scale, one infamous blockade for the OpenVPN service is the Great Firewall of China (see `https://openvpn.net/archive/openvpn-devel/2004-11/msg00028.html` for more information).

TLS authentication

OpenVPN provides a mechanism using a set of pre-shared keys to cryptographically sign every packet between the server and client. The mechanism for this is the same secret key used for a static-key OpenVPN setup, as was the original release.

The advantage to this signature is two-fold. First, it helps prevent any sort of denial of service attack using cryptographic routines within TLS to overload an OpenVPN server. The OpenVPN process will quite simply drop any packet without a valid signature before the CPU-intensive handshake and key exchange operations take place.

As a second advantage, `--tls-auth` aids in preventing keying material disclosure. This is specifically helpful for vulnerabilities such as Heartbleed or DROWN. If a cipher is completely broken, it is possible to still snoop the traffic from OpenVPN because `--tls-auth` doesn't provide any additional cryptographic layers.

> You can read more about the Heartbleed and DROWN OpenSSL vulnerabilities by going to the following links:
>
> - **Heartbleed (CVE-2014-0160)**: `https://web.nvd.nist.gov/vie` `w/vuln/detail?vulnId=CVE-2014-0160`
> - **DROWN (CVE-2016-0800)**: `https://web.nvd.nist.gov/view/vuln/detail?vulnId=CVE-20` `16-0800`

While being an added layer of protection for your VPN, `--tls-auth` can also cause connectivity problems. If the key direction is incorrect, or the pre-shared keys are out of sync, your VPN clients will be unable to connect, and the errors will manifest as connectivity issues.

The OpenVPN manual suggests that the key direction should not be defined in the server and client configuration for simplicity. In this scenario, only one key is used for packet signatures on both sides of the connection. If set, the values can be only either 1 or 0, with the server set to one value, and all clients set to the other value.

The `--tls-auth` key can either be expressed inline to the configuration or be written to a file like the certificates. When using a file, the configuration will resemble the following:

```
tls-auth /path/to/file.key 0
```

The preceding example provides a path to the key file, and specifies a key direction of 0. If this was for the server, we would want to ensure the client side was set to 1. Either side can be either value as long as the opposite end is the other value.

When using an inline `tls-auth` key, it would look like the following example. Notice that to specify the key direction, there is a distinct `--key-direction` parameter value present:

```
key-direction 0
<tls-auth>
#
# 2048 bit OpenVPN static key
#
-----BEGIN OpenVPN Static key V1-----
5f6a01fc8ed629aad7b26e6c6b474e5b
4a5446d3c81df9fd619d0a685b56a4c7
2997d8e5906a152687441a89742604cb
a2eb51e68ef260507d6681b04e5932d4
f35699b1fce29269dc75199df9281ac0
bd85ac8f4d097e2b2abfd03854d91466
d026c72f0ebd14b76cd3688e52dd1475
8be2996a577b97c198c8130c4824e97c
dd82dde648203f26a172385e4a36cc1d
b8633c1f0bb8c7954db540357cb88f75
571a21c4dae02e4cea767abb36713d3e
1b863b6dc479cf4081e3929e0f3f26d3
fa503629b587e5be01c95bd16cd8ae70
abd902bb8b95dfdcbd2dc552ef3f3e9a
01bdbc0e8df849aa6fc0aed7de6ce718
f15b696eaf0daad496bbaf7b78c4f00a
-----END OpenVPN Static key V1-----
</tls-auth>
```

If the secret keys do not match or the key direction parameter is not set correctly, both set to 0, for example, there will be TLS key errors present in both the server- and client-side logs. On the client side, the error will look like the following:

TLS Error: local/remote TLS keys are out of sync: [AF_INET]192.168.19.37:1194 [0]

On the server side, you will see two messages, one identifying the packet error and another identifying the offending peer:

Authenticate/Decrypt packet error: packet HMAC authentication failed TLS Error: incoming packet authentication failed from [AF_INET]192.168.19.104:1194

Note that modification by inline network intrusion systems that change values to the packet headers may introduce problems because the packet signatures will not validate. If you are seeing this behavior and are confident that your configuration is correct, try completely removing these parameters and see if the problem goes away. If so, there may be a device in the line tampering with packets.

Routing

OpenVPN provides powerful routing capabilities allowing the network administrator to direct traffic from clients where it needs to go. These routes can place entire subnets behind specific client connections, through other routers on the server side, or out to the Internet. There are two distinct zones when discussing routing and VPNs. I like to classify them as internal and external.

Regardless of which bucket your routes go into, it is vitally important to consider that both endpoints in the route need to know how to reach the other. There are varying techniques for accomplishing this: static routes, dynamic routes, NAT/PAT, and so on. Failure to ensure that there is a return path will prevent useful traffic from flowing.

In the following example image, the OpenVPN server resides behind a port-forwarding network gateway. The LAN gateway, nor the LAN file server, however, know how to route the 10.8.0.0/24 network. The OpenVPN client is able to send traffic via the OpenVPN server to the file server on LAN. That file server then responds via the default gateway because it does not have a more specific route for the VPN subnet. At this point, the gateway will either drop it (It is bad practice to forward RFC 1918 traffic out to the Internet) or forward it, only to be discarded upstream as unreachable (see https://tools.ietf.org/html/rfc1918, section 3, paragraph 8):

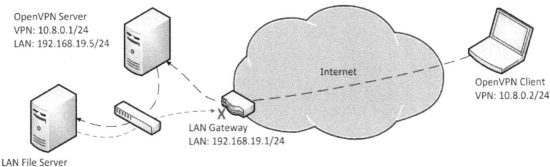

A missing return path causes overall communication failure

The simplest solution is to install a static route pointing the VPN subnet, 10.8.0.0/24, back to the VPN server at 192.168.19.5 on the LAN file server. If we are only dealing with a single or small handful of hosts, this might be the best option. In a corporate environment, where there are many hosts, however, this quickly becomes cumbersome.

The second option is to install the same route to the VPN subnet on the LAN gateway. This is generally less desirable, as it will cause the gateway to send an ICMP redirect message informing the LAN file server of the more direct route (via the VPN server). For a simple home network, this may be sufficient as some gateways may not have the routing features enabled to set static routes in a way accessible to the end user (homeowner/subscriber).

Another solution to return-path routing is to NAT VPN traffic from the VPN subnet out to the VPN server LAN address. This NAT method will result in all of the LAN systems only seeing the VPN server's LAN address, which they already know how to route because it is local. In the majority of cases, this should be sufficient. This does not work, however, if there are VPN resources that LAN clients want to access directly. We will discuss this in a later section.

One last method for resolving return-path routing is if the OpenVPN server is also the LAN gateway device. This is possible with only a few off-the-shelf residential gateways, and also a few commercial gateways, but there are some alternate firmware for some devices that allow for this. OpenWrt and pfSense are two examples of gateway devices firmware that embed OpenVPN.

When troubleshooting routing, the following flow chart is often referenced, and we consider it a gold standard for troubleshooting with regard to OpenVPN. The flowchart is designed to help troubleshoot routing when there are remote LANs/networks behind an OpenVPN client:

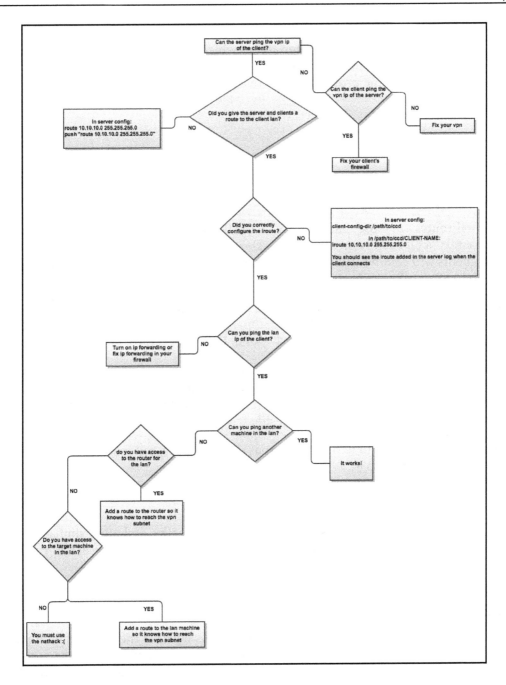

ICMP redirect (type 5) messages are sent when the next-hop for a routed packet is via the same interface on which the packet was received. Overall, this type of routing is inefficient, and it is better to route those packets directly to the proper host. More information about this is available at `http://www.cisco.com/c/en/us/support/docs/ip/routing-information-protocol-rip/13714-43.html` or at `https://ask.wireshark.org/questions/35826/what-does-icmp-redirect-redirect-for-host-mean`.

Internal routing

The **internal routes** are those that will stay inside the VPN. These do not pass outside the general context of OpenVPN or remain very close. In some configurations, the only thing the VPN clients will communicate with are either the VPN server (or some services hosted on the machine) or other VPN clients.

There are a few things that can go wrong with a simple setup like this. For example, let us set up an Apache server and run that on our OpenVPN server. Normally, users would connect to this web server over the normal system IP address (LAN or WAN is irrelevant).

With the server also running an OpenVPN server, however, the VPN clients must access the web server over the VPN IP or they could run into split routing. The server's public IP cannot be routed over the VPN. Access rules may allow additional privileges for VPN clients or provide virtual hosts that only reside within the VPN subnet.

There are no specific steps to verifying internal routing issues, but make sure the service you are trying to connect to is:

- Listening on the VPN IP address
- Providing the necessary access to the VPN clients
    - Database servers, protected web paths, and other similar services use IP addresses as one component to determine access rules

External routing

External routes are those that pass on to other networks whether they remain within the LAN/WAN or extend beyond out to the Internet. I see the external routes as the more complicated of the two as they generally involve cooperation of some sort from the other network.

A common use for passing external routes is to bypass geographical limitations enforced by various video streaming providers. Due to content licensing, translation, and local laws or regulations, access to various content is restricted for use based on their perceived geographical location based on the IP address. Many geolocation services attempt to place ranges of IPs within a physical location, often based on registration data (ARIN, APNIC, and others). Another more modern method is locating Wi-Fi access points based on GPS-enabled cellular phone records.

By connecting to a VPN server in a remote location, a user can appear (and functionally does) to originate from a different location than where they physically reside. Some of these content providers have gone to great lengths recently to restrict known VPN providers from access at all.

Pushing routes

When the admin wants VPN clients to connect to more than other VPN clients, it is generally necessary to push additional routes to those clients. These routes can be both internal and external to the VPN and can even include other OpenVPN processes. System administrators, for example, may connect to a different set of VPN servers than normal users.

Routes can reside behind other clients, static systems on the server LAN, external to the server LAN, or even be a new default route.

Routes behind clients

Through `--iroute` statements, OpenVPN can be made aware of routes behind clients, creating a route in the internal routing table. This is useful when you have a central office and one or more remote offices, for example. Each office should have its own subnet. The gateway device or a router behind it will have a VPN process that may act as a client to the central office's OpenVPN server.

The `--iroute` statement must be placed in a client-specific configuration file within `--client-config-dir` or CCD. If you place this directive in the general server configuration, it will be applied to all clients connected, rather than the single, correct, client. If the intent is to only have VPN clients route these subnets, there is no reason to add this to the kernel routing table (mentioned later).

Applying the `--push route "..."` to clients, along with `--iroute` in the correct CCD file, you can successfully traverse the VPN in to remote client subnets, without affecting the OpenVPN server itself. It is important to remember that the OpenVPN server can push routes to clients, but there is nothing to push those routes to the OpenVPN server. It is a good rule of thumb that for every pushed route, there should be a route in the server configuration, and vice versa.

Kernel versus process routing

There are two distinct routing tables on an OpenVPN server: the OpenVPN process internal routing table and the kernel routing table. Normally, in a simple OpenVPN setup with no additional routes, there is an interface route within the kernel routing table for the VPN subnet.

Both the `--route` and `--iroute` configuration arguments create routing table entries. The former propagates those routes to the kernel routing table, whereas the latter only tracks the routes internal to the OpenVPN process. The distinction is that if the kernel is unaware of a given route, LAN clients behind that OpenVPN system will be unable to reach those subnets. Likewise, a route can be placed within the kernel routing table, which will pass that route to the OpenVPN system, but the process needs to know to which client that goes in order to process it.

There are three primary steps to establish a full route within OpenVPN:

1. Establish process-specific routes (`--iroute`).
2. Apply necessary kernel routes (`--route`).
3. Push routes to clients (`--push "route ..."`).

In order for kernel routes that route across interfaces to be honored, IP forwarding needs to be enabled. This allows the system kernel to forward packets from one interface to another. Without this set, traffic routing will stop dead at the kernel. Both *nix and Windows have the concept of IP forwarding.

Modern Linux and Unix systems have `sysctls` or system controls that define some runtime kernel options. Most will use a separate IPv4 and IPv6 setting, `net.inet.ip.forwarding` and `net.inet6.ip6.forwarding`. These will vary somewhat, but good bet to find them shown here:

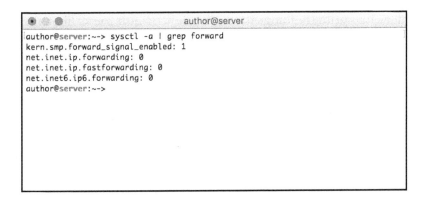

```
author@server
author@server:~-> sysctl -a | grep forward
kern.smp.forward_signal_enabled: 1
net.inet.ip.forwarding: 0
net.inet.ip.fastforwarding: 0
net.inet6.ip6.forwarding: 0
author@server:~->
```

For Windows, there is a similar mechanism within the system registry. You can find the necessary keys in
`HKEY_LOCAL_MACHINE\SYSTEM\CurrentControlSet\Services\Tcpip\Parameters` as the value `IPEnableRouter`. You can reference
`https://support.microsoft.com/EN-US/kb/230082` for further details.

Route conflicts

Be careful when selecting the IP range to use for your VPN. There are a couple of common home network subnets (`192.168.0.0/24` and `192.168.1.0/24`) that should never be used for a VPN. Other corporate ranges should also be avoided, like anything in the *10/8* subnet. Most importantly, make sure that whatever you're using doesn't conflict with what you want to connect to.

Redirect gateway

Many VPN providers will push a new default route to their client systems. Some third-party OpenVPN client GUIs will even go so far as to provide an option that notifies the user if the apparent external IP doesn't change once connected to a VPN.

Routes are followed by the most specific route and then by the routing metric. In general, OpenVPN routes all will have the same metric, so specificity matters. If OpenVPN actually replaced the core default route, the client would be unable to talk to the gateway, causing the connection to drop.

To push a new default gateway to OpenVPN clients, the `--redirect-gateway` configuration directive is provided. With the `def1` flag, all network traffic except local LAN traffic will be routed to the VPN server, even Internet-bound traffic such as web browsing.

This directive does two primary things to create a new default route. First, it creates a static route for the OpenVPN server, pointing to the current default gateway. Second, it creates two less-specific routes functionally providing a new default, without deleting the original route.

As I stated earlier, the routing table will follow the most specific route first. The normal default route is defined with the subnet `0.0.0.0/0`. This subnet includes all IPs. OpenVPN, to create more specific routes, applies `0.0.0.0/1` and `128.0.0.0/1`. These define the first half of the IPv4 address space, then the second half of the IPv4 address space.

Because these two routes are more direct than the initial default, they are chosen in favor, causing all traffic to flow to the OpenVPN server. The server still needs to route traffic from the clients to the general Internet.

Routing VPN traffic from clients out to the general Internet is often hidden behind a single IP address. The technique is named NAT. This masquerades all outbound traffic, regardless of origin, to a set of external IPs. Since your VPN will be composed of RFC 1918 addresses, they would be dropped by upstream routers. Besides this, many networks share the same common subnets, so the Internet routers would be confused and uncertain about where to send that traffic.

The OpenVPN server needs to NAT the VPN client traffic, and IP forwarding needs to be enabled.

General network concerns

Apart from routing, there are a few additional networking components that tend to trip up even some advanced server administrators.

Path MTU and MSS

Maximum transmission unit (MTU) problems are some of the most difficult problems to identify. In part, this is due to the odd symptoms that arise when an MTU incompatibility is present. During such a condition, some traffic will seem to function without a problem, whereas other traffic will inexplicably fail.

MTU is the largest packet that can traverse a network link intact. In the event that a larger packet transfer is attempted, it will either fail to reach the remote endpoint, or a fragmentation request will be sent back to the sender. This request tells the previous hop that the packet was too big and specifies how big the next packet should be:

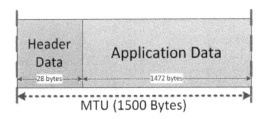

In general, when MTU problems exist, traffic with typically small packets will work without any issue. SSH, for example, sends many small packets during console sessions, often only a few keystrokes in an encrypted format. In my simple test, for example, the text a\n (the letter a followed by a newline) shows up across the wire as a 2-byte data segment. The same traffic generates 72 bytes of encrypted data:

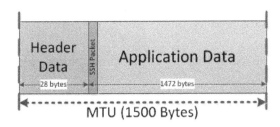

Note the relatively small amount of space used by the SSH packet

Because these packets have so little real data, there is little risk of exceeding the MTU, even if it is relatively small. Larger transfers, like using SCP to send a file to a remote system, however, will use much more of the data segment. If the file being transferred is larger than the MTU, packets carrying file data will generally max out the data segment:

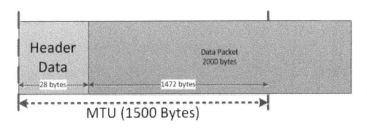

Data packet is too large for the available packet space

On normal Ethernet networks, the MTU is most commonly defined as 1500 bytes. All of the packet header data and application data must fit inside one of these packets. In the case of application data, larger chunks may be broken up across multiple packets:

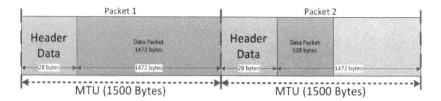

The same 2000 byte data split between two separate packets

There is inherent cost to processing packets for a switch or a router, as each packet must have its headers analyzed, a decision made on routing, and then outputting that packet where it needs to go.

With OpenVPN, additional encapsulation is added, which reduces the useful size of the overall data space in a given packet. The following diagram is simplified slightly from the real world, but the concept applies. When a packet is encapsulated within another, the entire child packet, including headers, must fit within the application data space:

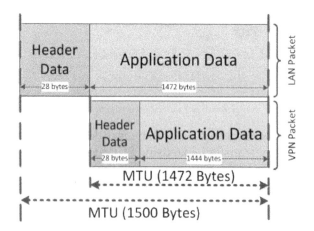

VPN data space is reduced per packet compared with a local network packet

Fortunately, OpenVPN comes prepacked with a tool you can leverage to identify the proper MTU for your VPN, `--mtu-test`. By adding the `--mtu-test` option to your configuration or passing it on the command line, OpenVPN will attempt to calculate the largest packet your VPN is capable of processing.

The ping command can be very useful in determining MTU, but there are a lot of different implementations of ping across different platforms. Essentially, using the following examples, depending on your OS of choice, you can send varying ping packets until a size is reached that begins to emit fragmentation needed or packet too large messages.

The BSD (on both OS X and FreeBSD) ping has some *sweeping* options for the packet size argument. This allows you to, without the need for an external `for-loop`, gradually increase the packet size until one begins to fail:

```
● ● ●                          author@client
author@client:~->: ping -G 1500 -g 1350 -h 10 -D 192.168.80.1
PING 192.168.80.1 (192.168.80.1): (1350 ... 1500) data bytes
1358 bytes from 192.168.80.1: icmp_seq=0 ttl=64 time=27.705 ms
1368 bytes from 192.168.80.1: icmp_seq=1 ttl=64 time=24.556 ms
1378 bytes from 192.168.80.1: icmp_seq=2 ttl=64 time=75.942 ms
1388 bytes from 192.168.80.1: icmp_seq=3 ttl=64 time=28.974 ms
1398 bytes from 192.168.80.1: icmp_seq=4 ttl=64 time=112.858 ms
1408 bytes from 192.168.80.1: icmp_seq=5 ttl=64 time=31.069 ms
1418 bytes from 192.168.80.1: icmp_seq=6 ttl=64 time=26.962 ms
1428 bytes from 192.168.80.1: icmp_seq=7 ttl=64 time=27.757 ms
1438 bytes from 192.168.80.1: icmp_seq=8 ttl=64 time=34.029 ms
1448 bytes from 192.168.80.1: icmp_seq=9 ttl=64 time=28.523 ms
1458 bytes from 192.168.80.1: icmp_seq=10 ttl=64 time=27.340 ms
1468 bytes from 192.168.80.1: icmp_seq=11 ttl=64 time=35.972 ms
1478 bytes from 192.168.80.1: icmp_seq=12 ttl=64 time=29.770 ms
ping: sendto: Message too long
ping: sendto: Message too long
Request timeout for icmp_seq 13
ping: sendto: Message too long
Request timeout for icmp_seq 14

--- 192.168.80.1 ping statistics ---
16 packets transmitted, 13 packets received, 18.8% packet loss
round-trip min/avg/max/stddev = 24.556/39.343/112.858/24.735 ms
author@client:~->
```

Using a ping on OS X to find the usable MTU

In this case, the command provides a maximum sweep (-G) we set to `1500`, a minimum sweep (-g) set to `1350`, the increase interval (-h) set to 10 bytes, and an option to set the **Do Not Fragment** bit. At a spacing of 10 bytes, our largest usable MTU would be `1470` (1478 – 8-bit ICMP header).

On Linux systems, you could write a `for-loop` to increase packet size for your selected bounds. Such a script might look like the following shell script:

Linux shell script looping through various packet sizes to find MTU

Finally, on Windows, we use a simple manual increment and run the ping command until it fails:

Windows manual test, incrementing until packet failure

Now that we know our magic number is 1478, we can use the `--fragment` and `--mssfix` configuration parameters to resolve packet size problems. The `--fragment` option forces the OpenVPN process to handle packet fragmentation for UDP packets. In our case, if we were experiencing packet loss for larger payloads, we would add `--fragment 1472` to our configuration. We can also add `--mssfix` to notify TCP connections of our reduced MTU, which will offload the packet fragmentation to the application or client system, reducing the load on the OpenVPN process.

Summary

This chapter covered some deep details about how to troubleshoot core network issues. Some tools, including Wireshark and `netcat`, were demonstrated, and the reader should be able to use these tools with some confidence. Like any tool, practice makes perfect, so I encourage you to use these for troubleshooting, investigation, and learning.

This chapter also provided some knowledge and reasoning behind how these technologies work. By understanding some of the theory behind the technology, it's my hope that you will be better prepared when finding and resolving a problem.

8
Performance

In a perfect scenario, your VPN users will have high-speed, dedicated connections over some sort of *hard line* to reach your server. Not only that, these same users will have top-end systems, equipped with an exorbitant amount of RAM, and high clock-speed CPUs equipped with the latest crypto-offload chipsets.

In reality, however, there are a variety of remote locations and devices that users will leverage to connect to a VPN. Some of these are out of necessity, such as a high-latency satellite connection, and others are out of convenience, such as using a mobile device. For the majority of your users, you should be able to provide sufficient cryptographic protections while still maintaining a comfortable performance level.

Networking

Network components on the client and server LAN can greatly affect the overall performance of the client-server connection. If the client is used in `--iroute`, other client connections to the distant LAN will also be affected.

Physical problems, such as improperly terminated fiber connections, poorly crimped RJ45 ends, and frayed or split Ethernet cables can introduce noise, resulting in packet transmission errors.

Network congestion from other LAN systems or uplink usage will not be readily apparent from within the VPN.

Rate limiting

Prior to around 2010, Internet connections were considered more or less a simple pipe in the consumer world. If you were given a 10 **Mbps** (**megabits per second**) connection, you were allowed to use the entirety of that connection for the duration of the month (or billing cycle). Commercial connections have long been treated in an entirely different manner.

For commercial connection, hosting, or uplink, the bandwidth has been metered in some regard for quite some time. There are a couple of ways you can purchase this bandwidth. First, you can purchase a dedicated *pipe*, which allows you to fully use that connection for the entire billing period. If you're paying for 10 Mbps, you can use all 10 Mbps, 24 hours per day, every day.

Another metering method, named **95th percentile**, can also be used. In this scenario, a business may order a 10 Mbps uplink, but pay a rate based on 1 Mbps. This means that the customer can use 1 Mbps the entire time, with no additional charge. Because the *pipe* is larger than 1 Mbps, this customer may burst to faster speeds for a potentially added rate. This burstability is where the 95th percentile measurement comes from; the top 5% of traffic is lopped off/ignored, and the customer is billed for everything less.

For the consumer market, Internet service providers have opted, instead, to institute bandwidth caps that are based on an aggregate of consumed transfer. This allows the consumer to use the full or maximum speed available when it is needed. This bandwidth cap started with cellular data plans. Once it was reached, the provider would rate limit the customer to a slower speed, typically around 144 Kbps (also known as 3G speeds), until the next billing cycle.

Rate limiting is an artificial limit to the physical or technical capabilities of a specific platform or system. These limits can be difficult to diagnose because there is nothing informing the user of this state. In the case of a VPN connection, the link can go quite suddenly from a satisfactory speed down to an unusable speed or one that is considered unusable by many people by today's standards.

There are tools that, if used sporadically over a period of time, can help identify when rate limiting has kicked in. This will only work when there is a change of rate limiting and not when it is a state common to every-day traffic.

First, there are sites such as **Speedtest** (`http://speedtest.net`) that allows you, using only a standard web browser, to determine your real-world transfer speeds. I tend to think of this as a good test since it shows a real transfer between a client system *somewhere* on the Internet out to another test system somewhere else on the Internet. In this case, the data transfer traverses your ISP and the ISP of the server host, demonstrating an end-to-end transfer.

There are other, similar tests available to customers of various ISPs. **CenturyLink**, for example, provides a supposedly more-direct test to your ISP's hosted test server. Running this test from the Speedtest server, a **Slashdot** server, and the CenturyLink server show odd results. The test is for my own personal home Internet connection, and it is executed outside a VPN. The purpose of this test is to see what the performance of the uplink is before we add the complexity of a VPN.

The first test is executed from the Speedtest website, which actually uses a server hosted on CenturyLink's network. This test results in an abysmal **30.66 Mb/s** download speed and a **491.71 Mb/s** upload speed. Neither is close to my paid for speed of 1 Gbps:

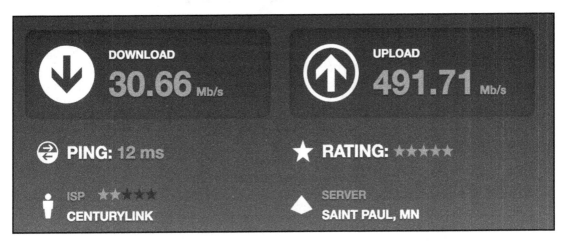

Speedtest result

The second result is a courtesy of `http://Slashdot.org/speedtest/` and shows marginally better results. I see a **347 Mbps** download speed, 11 times faster, and **197 Mbps** upload, 40% of the Speedtest result:

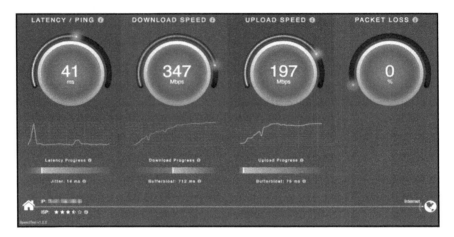

Slashdot result

Disappointingly, and despite a wired connection to my home router, I'm unable to realize the full potential of the connection I pay for. Based on these tests, I plan on reaching out to CenturyLink to identify the bottleneck. I have been told by various network engineers that the oversubscribed rate is about 12-1. Knowing that, I shouldn't expect to see my full billed rate 100% of the time, but I think it should be better than 50%:

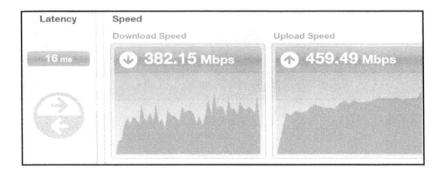

CenturyLink speed test result

Cryptographic performance

Cryptographic algorithms are complex mathematical formulas that require powerful microprocessors and good **entropy** (random data). The more advanced and complex an algorithm is, the more complex calculation will become. Older, slower processors will take substantially longer than newer and faster processors.

Library differences

Both OpenSSL and mbed TLS are constantly making improvements to both security and performance. While writing this book, I was using my MacBook Pro with the latest version of macOS (10.12.2) and I was going to show performance numbers for the AES cipher set using the `openssl speed -evp aes-128-cbc` command. The purpose is to show a reproducible performance metric on various platforms.

As you can see in the following screenshot, my Mac has OpenSSL version 0.9.8zh installed. OpenSSL included support for AES-NI with version 1.0, and the performance gains are evident in the first set of table entries (in the *Result summary* section, given later).

Performance results for mbed TLS are not included here since there are no easy-to-use cross-platform utilities available:

```
author@client:~-> which openssl
/usr/bin/openssl
author@client:~-> openssl version
OpenSSL 0.9.8zh 14 Jan 2016
author@client:~-> openssl speed aes
To get the most accurate results, try to run this
program when this computer is idle.
Doing aes-128 cbc for 3s on 16 size blocks: 35570036 aes-128 cbc's in 3.00s
Doing aes-128 cbc for 3s on 64 size blocks: 9349814 aes-128 cbc's in 3.00s
Doing aes-128 cbc for 3s on 256 size blocks: 2353870 aes-128 cbc's in 3.00s
Doing aes-128 cbc for 3s on 1024 size blocks: 588339 aes-128 cbc's in 3.00s
Doing aes-128 cbc for 3s on 8192 size blocks: 74087 aes-128 cbc's in 3.00s
Doing aes-192 cbc for 3s on 16 size blocks: 30401807 aes-192 cbc's in 3.00s
Doing aes-192 cbc for 3s on 64 size blocks: 8000796 aes-192 cbc's in 3.00s
Doing aes-192 cbc for 3s on 256 size blocks: 2012956 aes-192 cbc's in 3.00s
Doing aes-192 cbc for 3s on 1024 size blocks: 513760 aes-192 cbc's in 3.00s
Doing aes-192 cbc for 3s on 8192 size blocks: 63469 aes-192 cbc's in 3.00s
Doing aes-256 cbc for 3s on 16 size blocks: 26569004 aes-256 cbc's in 3.00s
Doing aes-256 cbc for 3s on 64 size blocks: 7036132 aes-256 cbc's in 3.00s
Doing aes-256 cbc for 3s on 256 size blocks: 1742877 aes-256 cbc's in 3.00s
Doing aes-256 cbc for 3s on 1024 size blocks: 447951 aes-256 cbc's in 3.00s
Doing aes-256 cbc for 3s on 8192 size blocks: 54663 aes-256 cbc's in 3.00s
OpenSSL 0.9.8zh 14 Jan 2016
built on: Oct  5 2016
options:bn(64,64) md2(int) rc4(ptr,char) des(idx,cisc,16,int) aes(partial) blowfish(idx)
compiler: -arch x86_64 -fmessage-length=0 -pipe -Wno-trigraphs -fpascal-strings -fasm-blocks -O3 -D_REENTRANT -DDSO_DLFC
N -DHAVE_DLFCN_H -DL_ENDIAN -DMD32_REG_T=int -DOPENSSL_NO_IDEA -DOPENSSL_PIC -DOPENSSL_THREADS -DZLIB -mmacosx-version-m
in=10.6
available timing options: TIMEB USE_TOD HZ=100 [sysconf value]
timing function used: getrusage
The 'numbers' are in 1000s of bytes per second processed.
type             16 bytes     64 bytes    256 bytes   1024 bytes   8192 bytes
aes-128 cbc    189699.08k   199176.48k   200787.21k   200551.31k   202035.70k
aes-192 cbc    161927.93k   170461.93k   171545.23k   175395.69k   173304.83k
aes-256 cbc    141506.31k   149907.52k   148539.98k   152712.42k   149300.87k
author@client:~-> clear
```

Cipher and AES-NI

In 2008, Intel and AMD released an extension to the x86 instruction set that improved encryption and decryption workloads that used **Advanced Encryption Standard** (**AES**).

 You can read additional information about AES-NI on Wikipedia at `https://en.wikipedia.org/wiki/AES_instruction_set`. If you are looking for more specific information about the instruction set, take a look at the development information available on Intel's website, `https://soft ware.intel.com/en-us/blogs/2012/01/11/aes-ni-in-laymens-terms`.

Result summary

I've published some results for the `aes-128-cbc` cipher test with a few versions of OpenSSL and highlighted the highest performers for overall. This is by no means a scientific test, and I encourage you to perform your own testing to determine what cipher works best for your hardware systems.

The numbers in the results indicate how many iterations were completed in a three-second loop for a given block size of data. Using the first row as an example, the Core i7 processor with 0.9.8zh OpenSSL processed a 64-byte block of data 119,176 k (119,176,000) times in three seconds:

Processor	OpenSSL	AES-NI	64b	256b	1024b	8192b
Core i7	0.9.8zh	No	199176k	200787k	200551k	202035k
	1.1.0c	No	155980k	167962k	164110k	169149k
	1.1.0c	Yes	850780k	881499k	870568k	791729k
Xeon E5620	1.0.1p	No	74303k	76464k	159140k	161211k
Xeon E5-2667 (VM)	1.0.1s	No	148654k	150422k	320264k	272821k
	1.0.1s	Yes	713594k	689075k	628269k	606528k
Xeon E5-2667	1.0.1t	No	118538k	120478k	129010k	121615k
	1.0.1t	Yes	575961k	778077k	799980k	669006k
Xeon E5-2620	1.0.1s	No	114402k	116569k	117204k	117861k
	1.0.1s	Yes	568017k	579300k	583670k	584672k
Xeon E5420	1.0.1s	No	78946k	80695k	169830k	174044k

	1.0.1s	Yes	208732k	215091k	217418k	217629k
Xeon E5-2640 v3	1.0.1e	No	148663k	152249k	152971k	153944k
	1.0.1e	Yes	350461k	354483k	357717k	356810k

There are a few notable results in the preceding table. First, the Xeon E5-2620 through VMware with a FreeBSD 10.3 system. Despite the virtualization involved, the raw throughput was right on par with the performance of bare-metal systems. For the Xeon E5-2667 results, I have posted data for both virtualized and bare-metal. The results are so close, it is difficult to tell if the performance delta is due to virtualization or the minor version difference between the VM and host system.

Single thread

A final, significant item to note is that OpenVPN is single-threaded (inclusive of OpenVPN 2.4). Regardless of how many processors or threads provided by the CPU, OpenVPN will be limited to a single thread. In various tests in recent years, a realistic limit of about 200 client connections is considered the maximum before performance falls off considerably.

It is possible to work around this limitation using load balancing across multiple OpenVPN server instances. These scenarios are more complicated as they require the administrator do additional configuration to ensure the two (or more) instances are able to communicate and clients are able to connect to the appropriate server(s).

The inclusion of AES-NI helps with this single-threading, as the cryptographic operations can be offloaded, speeding up the processing of each packet. On slow systems and those systems that do not include crypto-offloading, performance will be significantly slower.

Summary

There are a number of different factors that can affect the performance of your VPN. Some of these components will affect the client or server independently, but the overall VPN functionality will be influenced. Network conditions on the hosting Internet service provider, CPU and resource availability, and transport technology are but a few things to look at when troubleshooting performance problems.

In this chapter, I have illustrated some tools that can help determine performance as well as provided hints as to what can lead to performance degradation. At this juncture, you should be able to identify these items, along with many that were not mentioned.

Your troubleshooting should concentrate on the things you can quantitatively test and measure, followed by those components or variables you have control of.

9
External Problems

OpenVPN, by itself, can be a complex system, with given certificates, keys, configuration, scripts, hardware, and so on. The previous eight chapters of this book have touched on troubleshooting techniques and points on where to look within OpenVPN to address problems. However, once all the internal problems have been addressed, there are still several external influencers that can create additional hassles for your VPN.

Troubleshooting external factors for many things can be a difficult endeavor. In most cases, you'll be looking into a veritable black box for which you don't have a key. By setting up a VPN server, you are relying upon your **Internet Service Provider (ISP)** to allow transit for your VPN traffic on both the server and client side of the connection.

Inspection and filtering

Whether you are operating a server as a corporate tool or setting up a system to escape a *hostile* environment, there may be network policies in place that may prevent the successful operation of an OpenVPN connection. If you are a user on a large corporate or government network, it may be against usage policy to create a VPN tunnel and technology may be deployed to actively thwart such a tunnel.

Both corporate network administrators and many governments around the world are doing something named **Deep Packet Inspection** (**DPI**). A traditional firewall will only look at what the protocol and port traffic is using and allow or deny the traffic. This method will not prevent someone from moving a service that is blocked to an allowed port to circumvent the firewall.

A firewall or border gateway enabled with DPI is able to look beyond just the protocol and port and actually look at what the traffic is. In some cases, this can be to ensure TLS traffic is actually taking place. The inspection can go further, looking for prohibited patterns of data such as social security or credit card numbers, password hashes, and more. The Great Firewall of China (aka Golden Shield Project) is a well-known example of DPI at a national scale, and is known to filter according to strict rules.

OpenVPN does not do anything to obfuscate, or hide, tunnel traffic. The encapsulated data is secure, but someone looking at the traffic will know there is an encrypted tunnel in place. Wireshark even has an OpenVPN protocol filter (see the Wireshark Wiki at `https://wiki.wireshark.org/OpenVPN` for additional information). The simplest analogy I can use is that of a locked tractor trailer. You know someone is transporting goods, of some sort, between two places, but without the key, you don't know what is inside the trailer.

There are a few unique ways an ISP or other transit provider may filter OpenVPN. First, many OpenVPN tunnels use the **Internet Assigned Numbers Authority** (**IANA**) assigned port of `1194`. The simplest firewall can simply restrict *udp/1194* and *tcp/1194* (or not allow them, in the case of default-deny policies).

To illustrate some of the traffic inspection capabilities, we can see in the following screenshot how Wireshark is able to identify the OpenVPN traffic in the data stream:

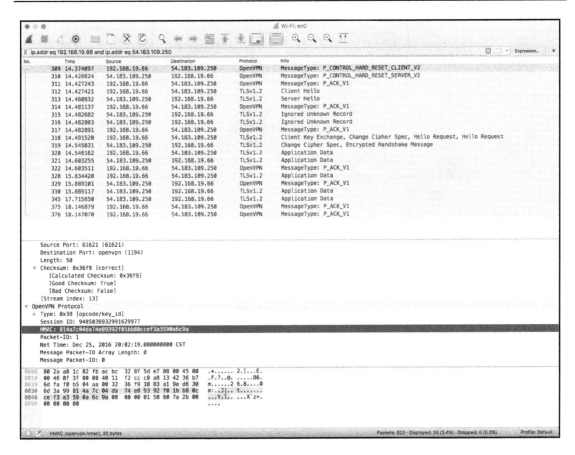

Wireshark recognizing the OpenVPN protocol and HMAC headers

If you suspect that your traffic is a victim of DPI, you can do a few things to test the theory.

The simplest test is to simply change the server port number away from the known OpenVPN ports (1194 and the older 5000). Initially, I suggest retaining the current protocol you're using, whether it be UDP or TCP. If your traffic begins working, it's possible that there is an explicit block of the OpenVPN ports. It may be useful to open a support ticket to request the port be opened or unblocked.

The next step in troubleshooting OpenVPN filtering is to attempt to piggy back on the outbound *tcp/443* firewall rule. Many organizations do not currently possess the means to perform full DPI, so we allow outbound HTTPS connections. In my experience, even some systems that do full inspection fail to follow the HTTPS stream so ignore, but do not block, the traffic.

 The intent of this section is not to encourage rogue network traffic or to enable a user to bypass normal security controls. In a hostile environment, this behavior may trigger other alerts however, attracting the attention of the network operator and further scrutiny.

Obfuscation

There is an apparent misunderstanding about the differences of encrypting data and hiding or anonymizing that data. These are two separate, distinct, concepts, and I feel that it needs to be cleared up for many novice VPN users.

First, let's discuss **obfuscation**.

> **obfuscate**: *1. to make dark or obscure 2. Confuse*
> *– The Merriam-Webster dictionary. Eleventh edition.*
> *2004. Print.*

The concept of obfuscation is to confuse, misdirect, or hide, VPN traffic. The idea here is to make the traffic blend in to the background in such a way as it appears as other, normal traffic. The end goal of these solutions is to completely hide the fact that a VPN is running at all.

In the wild, projects such as **obfsproxy** (`https://www.torproject.org/docs/pluggable-transports.html.en`) encapsulate VPN or other traffic inside an HTTPS tunnel, making it appear as normal web browsing. You can read more on using obfsproxy with OpenVPN on the community Wiki page at `https://community.openvpn.net/openvpn/wiki/TrafficObfuscation`.

Encryption

Now that we have defined obfuscation, we can move on to understanding **encryption**. Encryption is the act of coding something in such a way that only the sender and receiver understand the intended message, even if other parties can view, or overhear, the coded message.

> **encrypt**: *1: ENCIPHER*
> **encipher**: *to convert (a message) into cipher*
> **cipher**: *2a: a method of transforming a text in order to conceal its meaning*
>   *b: a message in code*
>
>   *– The Merriam-Webster website*

OpenVPN provides the encryption via the OpenSSL or PolarSSL libraries. Making use of static keys or certificate/key pairs provides a method to encode data within the tunnel in such a way that only the two endpoints can decrypt the data.

 Anonyproz has a decent write up about disguising OpenVPN traffic as HTTPS on their website at
`https://www.anonyproz.com/supportsuite/index.php?_m=knowledgebas`
`e&_a=viewarticle&kbarticleid=174.`

Geographic and source address exclusions

In the past couple of years, some online music and video streaming services have been known to block users based on their geographic location (**geo-blocking**). This blocking is accomplished using tools that lookup the known physical location of IP addresses, either via Wi-Fi router mapping (Google Maps, for example) or through registrar lookup data when more specific details are unknown.

Distribution licenses or agreements and local laws help determine where a distributor may want to make content available, even when the user base has a differing opinion on the matter. Almost as soon as geo-blocking was invented, users began using VPNs to work around these restrictions.

Services such as StrongVPN and HideMyAss popped up to defeat these blockages, promising users while traveling, or users that reside outside a distribution region, access to that content:

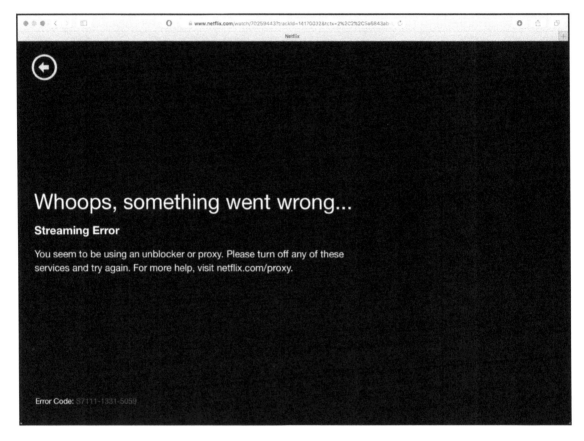

Netflix when attempting to bypass geo-blocking

What can be done

Fortunately, many hobbyists and home users will not see a problem with streaming services getting blocked when using a private VPN. There are a few things these providers look for to determine connection proxying.

Source IP address

The first thing that is looked at is the IP from where a streaming session is requested. Using **GeoIP** services, the provider will look up the known or assumed geographical location and base filtering on that data.

Through the use of a VPN, the user can change the apparent requesting IP to a location favorable for the desired content. For example, a user in Canada can *bounce* or route through a VPN system hosted in Dallas, Texas, to access USA-locked content, as shown in the following graphic:

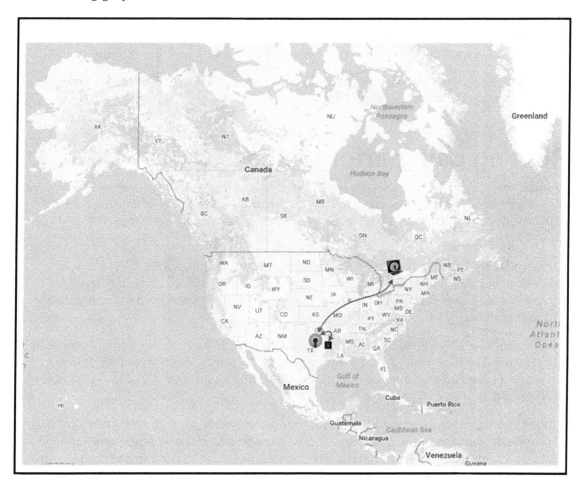

Routing streaming traffic through a VPN in another region

With a small number of users, this will likely work, where things will go sideways. However, if too many users begin using the same single IP address for streaming, the service provider will likely realize this behavior and begin blocking the content.

DNS settings

Content providers and **Content Distribution Networks** (**CDNs**) alike use DNS, along with some tricks using BGP, to point systems to a local cache server. This saves on transit costs, overall, for both the CDN as well as the ISP hosting the cache.

In my failed attempt, described previously, I used only a DNS provider to change my apparent location and the Netflix servers were able to see my apparent proxy. This was due to my DNS query result differing from my IP route.

When using geographically sensitive DNS queries, ensure that the DNS queries originate from the locations that will be requesting the data.

Routing path performance

Another component that is generally outside the control of a network operator is the overall network path. Peering agreements between upstream providers will determine the final path traffic with traverse. This path will often be weighted toward monetary cost and not always network path cost.

For many years, I ran the network for a small company in Minneapolis, MN, with the majority of our customers being local to Minneapolis. On occasion, I would receive complaints of slow performance of our network as customers attempted to communicate with our systems.

After troubleshooting, we would identify a slow hop in the path between their systems and our systems. The most frustrating part was, physically, our facilities were only 10 or so miles apart (16 km), but the network path would go approximately 400 miles (645 km) to Chicago and another 400 miles back.

At the time, due to our hosting situation, we did not have the tools or agreements in place to change the network routing. Eventually, we were able to make an agreement with the Midwest Internet Cooperative Exchange (http://micemn.net). Using this exchange, other ISPs connected to the exchange, large and small, would keep local traffic local.

As a VPN administrator, it may be useful to consider the geographic needs of the business or use and route traffic sensibly. Some useful tools, such as `mtr`, were presented in `Chapter 1`, *Troubleshooting Basics*. Knowing how traffic is routed for your customers and clients will reduce potential performance problems.

Summary

The most basic VPN tunnel, like the one created using the **Static Key Mini-Howto** (`https://openvpn.net/index.php/open-source/documentation/miscellaneous/78-static-key-mini-howto.html`), involves only a few components and can be relatively easy to troubleshoot. As functionality and capability is added, however, additional components are leveraged, which will require their own set of troubleshooting techniques. By writing *Troubleshooting OpenVPN*, it was my goal to provide two specific, unique, sets of information.

The first tool is the OpenVPN specific knowledge and known issues presented here. This spans the breadth of issues identified by users on **Internet Relay Chat (IRC)**, the web forums (`https://forums.openvpn.net`), and the mailing list (`http://sourceforge.net/p/openvpn/mailman/`). These are the most common occurring problems or sticking points encountered by both experts and novices, alike.

The second tool I tried to provide is a more general technique for troubleshooting. This techniques applies to anything from fixing a broken lamp to a complex OpenVPN deployment. Throughout the book, I demonstrated splitting a failure into the functional components, how to identify what is working, and how to tackle the non-working piece.

As I'm finishing this book, the developers are working hard on the final release for OpenVPN 2.4 (as this is written, 2.4 release candidate 2 is already out). The new release has a long list of new features and enhancements. While exciting, these will all present their own troubleshooting and deployment challenges. You can check the release notes for 2.4 at `https://community.openvpn.net/openvpn/wiki/ChangesInOpenvpn24`.

Useful links

In case they were missed throughout the book, here's a list of some useful links related to the OpenVPN project.

Manual or man pages

The **manual** or **man** pages provide the detailed documentation of the various configuration parameters and limitations for configuration of OpenVPN. These documents will illustrate each given version's capabilities and how to use them. The man pages should be a first-resort reference. The various man pages are as follows:

- **2.0**:
  `https://openvpn.net/index.php/open-source/documentation/manuals/openvpn-20x-manpage.html`
- **2.1**:
  `https://openvpn.net/index.php/open-source/documentation/manuals/openvpn-21.html`
- **2.2**: `https://community.openvpn.net/openvpn/wiki/Openvpn22ManPage`
- **2.3**: `https://community.openvpn.net/openvpn/wiki/Openvpn23ManPage`
- **2.4**: `https://community.openvpn.net/openvpn/wiki/Openvpn24ManPage`

Release notes

For each release, the OpenVPN developers publish a change list and a set of release notes. Typically, these will document the most notable changes between the previous release and the current release. When upgrading, it is recommended to read through the entirety of release notes between your current version and the version to which you are upgrading. The various release notes are as follows:

- **2.0**:
  `https://openvpn.net/index.php/open-source/documentation/release-notes.html`
- **2.1**:
  `https://openvpn.net/index.php/open-source/documentation/change-log/changelog-21.html`
- **2.2**:
  `https://openvpn.net/index.php/open-source/documentation/change-log/45-open-source/change-log/425-changelog-for-openvpn-22.html`
- **2.3**: `https://community.openvpn.net/openvpn/wiki/ChangesInOpenvpn23`
- **2.4**: `https://community.openvpn.net/openvpn/wiki/ChangesInOpenvpn24`

Support channels

There are a few different sources of support available to you for the open source (aka community) version of OpenVPN. The mailing list is probably the most commonly used medium, but there can be a delay, like the forums, due to the asynchronous communication method. Often, however, you will receive a thoughtful and detailed reply. IRC offers the most real-time support option, but active users, versus those only *idling*, varies by time of day. Use whichever of the following you are most comfortable with:

- **IRC**: `https://freenode.net`, *#openvpn* and *#openvpn-devel*
- **Web forum**: `https://forums.openvpn.net`
- **Mailing list**: `https://sourceforge.net/p/openvpn/mailman/`
- **Bug tracker**: `http://community.openvpn.net/openvpn/report/1`
- **Source/contributions**: `https://github.com/openvpn/`

Index